THE DINOSAUR DILEMMA: FACT OR FANTASY

Volume VII
Creation Science Series

By Dennis Gordon Lindsay

Published by
Christ For The Nations Inc.
P.O. Box 769000
Dallas, TX 75376-9000

First Printing — 1990
Second Printing — 1998
(Revised and Expanded)

All Scripture NIV unless otherwise noted.

ACKNOWLEDGMENTS

A number of organizations have aided my research in preparing and producing this book. I wish to express special appreciation and acknowledgment to the following:

The Creation Life Publishers of San Diego, California; *Creation Ex Nihilo* magazine of Australia; Bible-Science Association of Minneapolis, Minnesota; Institute for Creation Research of El Cajon, California; The Genesis Institute of Richfield, Minnesota; Creation Evidences Museum of Glen Rose, Texas, and Films for Christ of Mesa, Arizona.

These organizations have been evangelical Christianity's foremost defenders of Creation Science. For their substantial contribution to my own life and ministry, I personally wish to thank them and their staffs. I highly recommend their materials to those who wish to keep abreast of the events in the ongoing struggle between the forces of light and darkness regarding the Creation Science-evolutionism issue.

FOREWORD

The purpose of the Creation Science Series is simply to make information available to all laypersons interested in the subject. My intent is to provide support for Creation Science that is easy to read and comprehend, while leaving out much of the technical jargon that only a specialist would appreciate. Those who desire additional information and documentation by experts in the Creation Science community may contact the following outstanding organizations:

MASTER BOOKS
  9260 Isaac St., Suite E
  Santee, CA 92071

INSTITUTE FOR CREATION RESEARCH
  2100 Greenfield Dr.
  P.O. Box 2667
  El Cajon, CA 92021

BIBLE-SCIENCE ASSOCIATION
  P.O. Box 33220
  Minneapolis, MN 55422-0220

CREATION EVIDENCES MUSEUM
  P.O. Box 309
  Glen Rose, TX 76043

GENESIS INSTITUTE
  7232 Morgan Ave S.
  Richfield, MN 55423

APOLOGETICS PRESS INC.
  230 Landmark Dr.
  Montgomery, AL 36117-2752

CREATION SCIENCE EVANGELISM
29 Cummings Rd.
Pensacola, FL 32503
Phone: (850) 479-3466

Cover design by Don Day, and illustrations by Diana Sisco Dorn and
Camille Barnes.

TABLE OF CONTENTS

Talk About Chemical Warfare! — A Look
at Bombies' Internal Combustion Chambers
— Six Conditions for Making Fire —
Strange Apparatus on Fossilized Dinosaurs
— Curious Heads — Artillery Skulls —
Who is King Today?

Why So Much Space? — The Message of
Behemoth and Leviathan — Job's Pride —
God Compares Job to the Unmanageable
Leviathan — The Pride of Mankind

How in the World? — Contrary to Public
Opinion

Have All Dinosaurs Died? — The Komodo
Dragons — The American Alligator —
Reptile Growth — Changing Definitions to
Save Face — Reptile Growth — The Post-
Flood World

Dragon Folklore — Ye Ol' Dragon —
Nimrod, the Mighty Hunter — Babylonia
(2000 B.C.) — Africa (Fourth Century B.C.)
— India (Third Century B.C.) — China —
Scandinavia — Early Britain — East
Anglica, England (A.D. Seventh Century) —
Ireland (10th Century) — Madagascar (13th

Figure #1. MEET THE DINOSAUR FAMILY

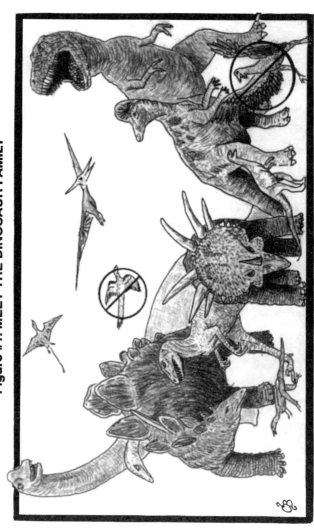

Introduction

(See fig. #1)

Fact or Fantasy?

From where did dinosaurs come? Did God create dinosaurs, or were they some genetic experiment of Satan? Were dinosaurs part of pre-Adamic creation? Did Noah take dinosaurs on the Ark? Did man and dinosaurs live at the same time? Are dinosaurs mentioned in the Bible? What were the creatures behemoth and leviathan spoken of in Scripture (Job 40:15; 41:1)? In Job 41:20, smoke and fire are discharged by leviathan. Is this merely symbolic? What are the spiritual implications of the great dinosaurs of the past? Have all dinosaurs died; and if so, why did they become extinct? What dinosaurs may still be alive today?

Dinosaur Hoopla. (See fig. #2.)

Dinosaurs have become a part of every child's life, and even adults have to admit to having a strange fascination about these sinister-looking creatures. The reason for the obsession with

Figure #2. MEGA-MONSTER MANIA

these monsters is not only that they are a villainous mystery, but the media has spawned widespread interest. There are continuous discoveries of fossilized remains of these creatures from different parts of the world, which inspire kids to imagine that the bones of one of these "nasty" creatures might just be in a nearby creek. Then there are the giant-screen movies which hit the theaters every so often, capturing the imaginations, as well as the pocketbooks, of millions of people. Hollywood has made fortunes off scary reptilian movies, and there will always be a new crop of youngsters who will enter the giant-screen cinema to be terrorized by the latest science fiction technology. This technology claims to have recreated mega-monsters from the DNA of a dinosaur.

How to Make a Dinosaur According to Hollywood.

The typical plot of these scary movies involves the extraction of the DNA code from dinosaur blood found in a frozen mosquito. Sixty-five million years earlier, the mosquito had sucked blood from a dinosaur in the tropical prehistoric world. Then the mosquito somehow made its way to a glacier in Siberia, where it then became trapped and frozen until the 21st century, where it was discovered by a scientist. After examining the mosquito in the laboratory, it was discovered that it contained the blood of an ancient reptilian lizard.

Shortly thereafter, a living giant reptilian beast is produced from the DNA. The dinosaur and its mate are sent to an isolated and deserted South Pacific island, where they can have an extended honeymoon. It doesn't take long before the mega-monster decides it has had enough "matrimony," and takes a 5,000-mile swim to the shores of California, where it goes searching for lunch. Failing to find a satisfactory meal, it becomes irritable and destroys half of Los Angeles. Continuing its search, it proceeds to cross the United States demolishing everything in its path until it arrives at New York City, where it brings unending havoc to the "Big Apple." **(See fig. #3.)** Somehow it manages to climb the World Trade Center Twin Towers, where it is eventually nuked, and peace once again returns to the world — until its mate decides to leave the island in the sequel movie, *Monster Mania II.*

Dinosaurs are big business, and are used to sell everything from baseballs, hot dogs and Chevrolets to grandma's homemade apple pie. They can be found in shops and flea markets in just about every size, shape and form imagin-

Figure #3. THE LIFE AND TIMES OF GODZILLA

able. Ultimately, they end up in closets or attics for another generation of kids to stumble on while exploring the dusty corners of their parents' homes.

Besides these "imaginary" dinosaurs, there are fossilized remains of real dinosaurs found on every continent. Many national and local museums house full-sized dinosaur replicas. So with all of the money to be made from these creatures, no doubt interest in them will be alive and well for centuries to come.

The Truth About Dinosaurs.

There has been an explosion of scientific discovery of dinosaur fossils over the last several decades. As a result, books are being published every month releasing new data about the kingdom of dinosaurs. This information being spread has led to many changes in people's thinking concerning dinosaurs — their looks, life, habits, history and extinction.

For decades, the Church wondered if such creatures actually existed; and even today, some ministers don't quite know how to handle the topic of dinosaurs, for they are unsure of just how they fit into the Bible.

The Dinosaur Dilemma: Fact or Fantasy will attempt to cover everything you have always wanted to know about dinosaurs but were afraid to ask your pastor.

Included in our study of the dinosaurs is a prophetic message which opens the door of understanding regarding these mega-monsters. The Bible reveals this spiritual lesson. There is something of eternal significance in the creation and the extinction of the dinosaurs which God desires His children to know and apply to their personal lives.

Before investigating this subject from a biblical perspective, a short history may be helpful, especially to those who will be sharing it with children or youth.

Chapter One

A Bit of Dinosaur History

The First Recorded Modern-Day Discovery of Dinosaur Fossils.

The first discoveries of dinosaur fossils were not even recorded since prehistoric monsters were considered to live only in overactive imaginations and in fairy tales. The few fossils which had been found were thought to have belonged to a giant animal, such as an elephant, and the footprints to some sort of gigantic bird.

But in 1822, the wife of an English doctor, Gideon Mantrell, was taking a walk while visiting in Lewes, Sussex, England. Among some rocks piled alongside the road, she saw what resembled a large tooth. Because her husband had an interest in fossils, she knew this could be important, and took it to him. Dr. Mantrell then hastened to the spot where his wife had found the tooth. There he discovered not only more teeth, but some bones as well — though not a complete skeleton. He believed that he had found an entirely new group of reptiles, and so he decided to send them to an expert on fossils, Baron Cuvier of Paris, France.

Cuvier mistakenly identified the teeth as being from an extinct rhinoceros, and the bones as belonging to an extinct hippopotamus. Dr. Mantrell was not satisfied with this explanation, and later discovered that the fossils resembled the bones and teeth of a Central American lizard — the iguana **(see fig. #4)** — though much larger, of course. He gave his discovery the name Iguanodon, meaning "iguana-tooth."

It was not until 1878 that another fossil find, this time in Belgium, made it possible to know what an Iguanodon really looked like. **(See fig. #5.)** There, in a coal mine, several dozen complete skeletons of Iguanodons were found piled together. Fossil bones and teeth of another ancient creature of the same kind, only at a different place, had by this time been found, though no complete skeleton had come to light. The great discovery in Belgium proved beyond any doubt that these monsters did indeed exist at one time on the Earth. From that point, fossils of prehistoric animals became a matter of intense interest and have been extracted from all over the world.

Figure #4. THE IGUANA LIZARD

Figure #5. MEET THE FIRST DINOSAUR: MR. IGUANODON

The Meaning of "Dinosaur."

The name dinosaur was coined by Sir Richard Owen in 1841 to describe an order of extinct giant reptiles in his address to the British Association for the Advancement of Science. He derived it from two Greek words meaning terrible (deinos) and lizard or reptile (sauros).

Since the first modern-day find of dinosaur fossils in 1822, there have been many additional finds. Today some books list as many as 200 different kinds of dinosaurs and one even has nearly 1,000 different kinds. However, the validity of this figure is somewhat dubious since many of these have been reconstructed from as little as one tooth. No doubt most of the 1,000 listed are cousins, related as are different breeds of dogs.

How to Fossilize a Dinosaur.

When fossils are found, there are always dozens of them — young and old — fossilized together. They are piled and jammed into stacks, showing evidence of having been suddenly caught in a violent disaster **(see fig. #6)** that deposited these carcasses, along with sediment, in huge layers. The sediment then hardened and preserved the bones.

Eventually, minerals in the ground water are

Figure #6. CAUGHT IN NOAH'S FLOOD

gradually deposited in the tiny network of holes running through the bones and teeth, completely filling them. After the water drains away and evaporates, the minerals harden, leaving a petrified fossil replica of the dinosaur bones and teeth. **(See fig. #7.)** Eventually, with the passing of hundreds or thousands of years, erosion may expose the fossil remains of the dinosaur making it possible for someone to discover them. The bones then can be excavated **(see fig. #8)** and studied and then reassembled so they can be housed in a museum. **(See fig. #9.)**

Found Everywhere. (See fig. #10.)

Evidences of dinosaurs have been found as far north as the Arctic islands, and recently a fossil graveyard of Duckbill dinosaurs **(see fig. #11)** was discovered above the Arctic circle in Alaska, proving dinosaurs existed very far to the north.

Dinosaur fossils also have been found as far south as the southern tip of South America and in Australia. Sometimes they have been found in massive fossil graveyards such as the Dinosaur Monument **(see fig. #12)** located in the northwest corner of Colorado and northeast corner of Utah. The museum in the park that houses the dinosaur fossils is a government-founded exhibition and does not present information from a biblical

Figure #7. HOW TO FOSSILIZE A DINOSAUR

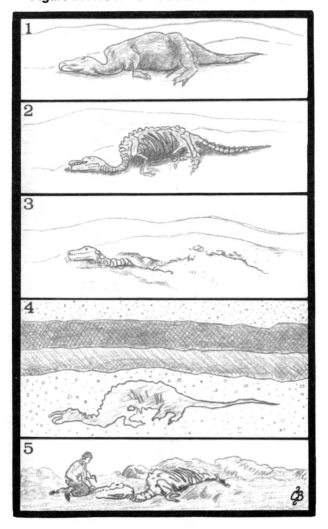

Figure #8. RESURRECTING A DINOSAUR FROM ITS GRAVE

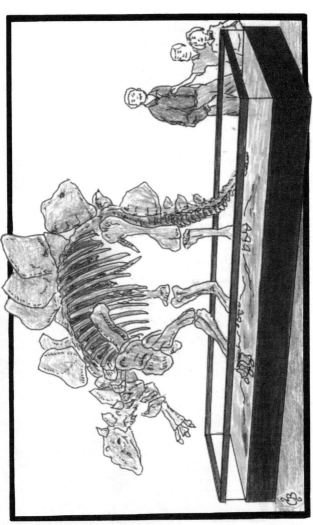

Figure #9. BONES OF BEHEMOTH

Figure #10. ROAMING THE EARTH

Figure #11. DUCKBILL DINOSAUR: SHANTUNGOSAURUS

Figure #12. JURASSIC BURIAL GROUNDS: DINOSAUR NATIONAL MONUMENT

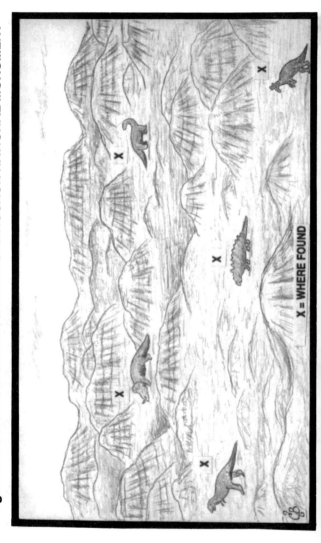

X = WHERE FOUND

perspective. However, the information does state that the thousands of dinosaur bones located in the park are a result of a flood catastrophe. Of course, this backs up the biblical position that the catastrophe that brought death to the dinosaurs was the worldwide flood known as the Genesis Flood.

Chapter Two

The Case of the Missing Identity

The Wrong-Headed Dinosaur.

For decades, one of the all-time favorite dinosaur was the Brontosaurus. **(See fig. #13.)** But, did you know that this fellow never existed — though pictures of it have been published in scores of science textbooks, many of its fossilized remains have been reassembled (from parts of other dinosaurs), and replicas have been displayed in museums around the world? How is all that possible if the Brontosaurus never existed?

Before explaining what happened, let me answer another question. How do scientists understand *anything* about dinosaurs?

Scientists gather information about dinosaurs from the fossilized remains they find in rocks. Literally, every part of many different kinds of dinosaurs has been unearthed. Not only have

Figure #13. BRONTO: THE NONEXISTENT DINO

their massive bones been uncovered, but their claws, teeth **(see figs. #14 & 15)**, horns, eggs **(see fig. #16)**, and on occasion, an unborn baby dinosaur. Even imprints from their skin **(see fig. #17)** have been discovered, as well as the remains of their last meal, preserved in their stomachs. Fos-

Figure #14. DINO MEMORABILIA:CLAWS

Figure #15. DINO MEMORABILIA: TEETH

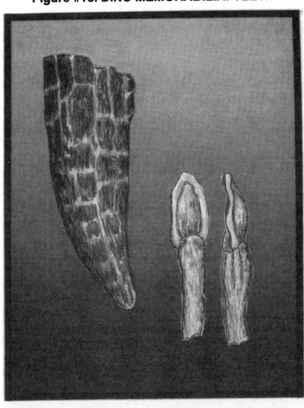

sils of dinosaur skin show they had thick, scaly skin, but we have no idea what colors they may have been. Footprints, the size of a bathtub **(see fig. #18)**, have been preserved by the thousands in the rocks around the world.

Figure #16. DINO MEMORABILIA: EGGS

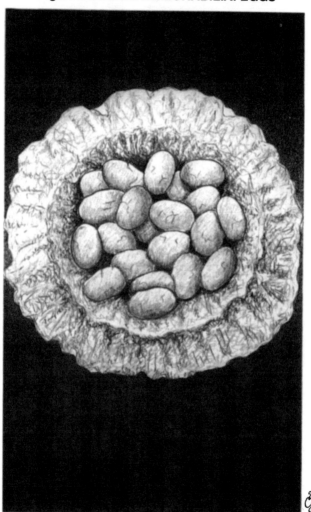

Figure #17. DINO MEMORABILIA: SKIN

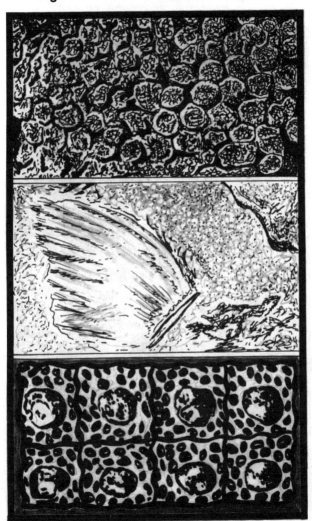

Figure #18. DINO MEMORABILIA:
BATHTUB FOOTPRINTS

Dinosaur investigation and research have undergone a revival in very recent years, and this has become a transitional period in which many of the previous conceptions about dinosaurs have been revised. The pieces of the dinosaur puzzle continue to change because no one has ever seen how the now extinct creatures actually appeared when they roamed the Earth.

Back to Bronto.

Now back to the rest of the story about the dinosaur that never existed. When the fossils of what came to be known as the Brontosaurus were first discovered, its head was missing. Since there were other dinosaur remains nearby, a skull was found and added to complete the skeleton. And Bronto Baby was born. For decades, it was a household word to millions of kids around the world. Unfortunately, Bronto's head belonged to a relative found some distance away from the resting place of Bronto's remains.

Recently, a complete skeleton of the missing relative was found, and it was discovered that the body of Bronto was actually that of Apatosaurus. The skull was from still another dinosaur known as Camarasaurus. **(See fig. #19.)** Although somewhat similar in appearance, museums around the world quickly made modifications to correct the

Figure #19. IMPOSTORS: CAMARASAURUS AND APATOSAURUS

error on their models of the creature. As a result, Brontosaurus quietly became "extinct" from all new textbooks. Bronto is one dinosaur that never made it onto Noah's Ark, but only onto the evolutionary ark that sank decades ago.

Speaking of Heads. (See fig. #20.)

Check out these curious heads. These creatures were famous for their odd-shaped heads. Their humps, bumps, crests and spines are made of thin hollow bone. Maybe they were the first snorkelers, or maybe they got together on a Saturday evening hoedown as an instrumental quintet. Could they have used their strange apparatus to make sounds — music? Remember, what is noise to one Pachycephalosaurus may be music to another.

The Evolutionism of Dinosaur Reconstruction.

Another example of mistaken identity involves the Iguanodon. When the Iguanodon was first discovered, it was thought it had a horn on its nose. Later it was found it had no horn on its nose, but a spike on each of its thumbs! These illustrations reveal the mistaken perceptions that people who reconstruct fossil bones often have. No wonder so many reassembly jobs have become jokes. **(See fig. #21.)**

Figure #20. THE KNUCKLEHEADS

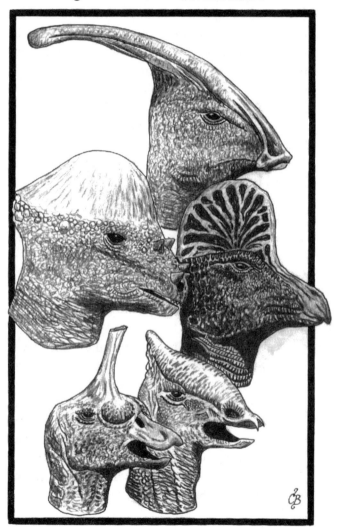

Figure #21. A BODY OVERHAUL

Puzzling Puzzles.

Attempting to assemble a dinosaur skeleton from bones discovered in a fossil graveyard is like trying to put together a 1,000-piece, 3-D jigsaw puzzle — without a picture, with many of the pieces missing, warped or mangled, and pieces from other puzzles mixed in. The massive weight of the layers of rock and dirt on fossilized bones often crushes and distorts the skeleton. There are many missing parts which often have to be concocted when assembling dinosaur bones to be housed in a museum. Often bones from many different dinosaurs, and even other creatures, are all put together.

As previously mentioned, dinosaurs have been reconstructed from less than 10 percent of their complete skeletal frame — some from a single tooth or bone. Thus, many of the descriptions of dinosaurs are based on guesswork, and are merely the product of human imagination.

No one knows exactly what dinosaurs looked like or the nature of these massive creatures. Both evolutionists and Hollywood producers have given us a distorted and biased viewpoint. Today when dinosaur fossils are discovered, most of the time they are correctly assembled anatomically. But when an attempt is made to reproduce the exterior features — such as muscle, fiber and skin thickness — one guess is as good as another. As a result, there is much speculation and conjecture involved.

An Elephant or One-Eyed Bigfoot?

For example, suppose elephants had long since become extinct, and no record of their physical characteristics had been made. Now imagine a scientist discovering the remains of some of the biggest elephants that ever lived. **(See fig. #22.)** Although the skeletal frame may be reconstructed correctly **(see fig. #23)**, all sorts of ideas about the nature and disposition could

Figure #22. 3-D PUZZLES

**Figure #23.
PUTTING THE
PIECES TOGETHER**

**Figure #24.
ERRONEOUS
CONCLUSIONS**

be theorized, especially about the huge ivory tusks. When it came to adding hair, flesh and muscle fiber, more comical concepts no doubt would be imagined. **(See fig. #24.)** And who would believe that these huge creatures could be so friendly to man, or that they could be trained to perform in circuses, sports events, or assist in construction projects? **(See fig. #25.)**

Suppose only a part of an elephant's fossil remains was found. An attempt at reconstruction could wind up pretty ridiculous. Suppose only the skull was found. **(See fig. #26.)** After adding some hair and flesh in the right places, one might even conclude that this was some hominoid creature such as a "One-Eyed Bigfoot." **(See fig. #27.)** Do you think this is a harebrained idea? Then consider Brachiosaurus.

Figure #25. ELEPHANTS: FRIENDLY SERVANTS OF MAN

Figure #26. SKULLDUGGERY

Figure #27. SKULL ABSURDITY: ONE-EYED BIGFOOT

The shape of a Brachiosaurus is still open for discussion. Some scientists think the huge nostrils on top of the Brachiosaurus' skull meant that it may have had a trunk **(see fig. #28)**, like that of an elephant. There are many surprises about dinosaurs yet to be realized by the public. Some interesting and little known facts are revealed in the next chapter.

Figure #28. BRACHIOPHANT

Chapter Three

Did You Know?

Did You Know That Most Dinosaurs Are Small?

When people think of dinosaurs, they think of the giant ones they have seen in movies or on display in a museum. However, not all dinosaurs were massive in size. Some, like the Saltopus, didn't grow much larger than a kitty cat. **(See fig. #29.)** Most dinosaurs were less than 15 feet long.

Did You Know That Many Dinosaurs Hatched From Small Turkey-Sized Eggs?

No one knows for sure whether or not all dinosaurs came from eggs, but we do know that many did. Most dinosaur eggs are just a bit larger than a turkey egg. Eggs from a 40-foot-long dinosaur, the Hypselosaurus, were discovered, and each egg was about a foot long. This means that newborn dinosaurs were very small. **(See fig. #30.)**

Figure #29. "PUSS"OSAURUS

Figure #30. DINO-MITES

It is obvious that the dinosaurs didn't reach their massive dimensions overnight. But reptiles continue to grow throughout their entire lifetime. So as long as they had a great deal of time, they could grow into giants. The Bible reveals that men lived for about 1,000 years before the great Flood of Noah's day. It would follow that all the creatures had similar life spans. In those times, dinosaurs would have enjoyed a relatively comfortable environment which supported a long and healthy growing season.

The fossil records reveal that in the past, everything grew larger, including animals, insects, birds, plants and mankind.[1]

Did You Know That Giant Dinosaurs Had Pea-Sized Brains?

Even more interesting is the tiny brain size of these immense creatures. For example, the 12-foot-tall, 30-foot-long, 20,000-pound Stegosaurus had a brain only about the size of a quarter. **(See fig. #31.)** The brain of the giant Apatosaurus (length: 70-100 feet; weight: 35 tons) was just slightly larger than that of a puppy dog. If it were possible to reduce the size of the gigantic Brachiosaurus to the size of a tall Texan, its brain would be smaller than a pea.

In other words, the large size of the dinosaurs

Figure #31. A WALNUT-SIZED BRAIN

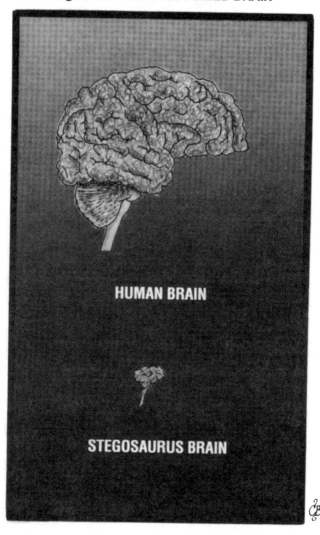

is no indication that they were more ferocious than if they were smaller. It may be that most dinosaurs were harmless plant-eaters, not much different in their habits than a giraffe, buffalo or elephant. **(See figs. #32A & B.)** More will be said about dinosaur temperaments in Chapters Thirty-Four through Thirty-Nine.

Did You Know That Many Dinosaurs Have Been Reconstructed From Only a Fragment of a Bone?

How many different dinosaurs were there? Evolutionary books on dinosaurs give the idea there were hundreds of different kinds of dinosaurs. However, when one makes a careful investigation, he finds there were far fewer dinosaurs than we have been led to believe. Many of the so-called dinosaurs may never have existed; they have been re-created from only a tooth or other small fragment. Here are some examples:

- Arctosaurus is known from only one vertebra.
- Colonosaurus is known only from a jaw, which could be from a bird or sea lizard.
- Diplotomodon is known only from one tooth.
- Paronychodon was named from a single tooth found in Montana.

Figure #32A. VEGETARIANS

Figure #32B. VEGETARIANS

- Chienkosaurus is known from just four teeth. Some experts think they came from a prehistoric crocodile.
- Embasaurus is known only from a few pieces of bone.
- Macrodontophion is known from just one round-topped tooth.
- Supersaurus is possibly a diplodocid.
- Dystrophaeus is known only from pieces of bone from an arm, hip, or shoulder. It was a big dinosaur, possibly the same kind as another already named.
- Aepisaurus is from one arm bone found in France.

It seems that every time bone fragments are found in rock, someone comes up with a new dinosaur! Some complete skeletons of dinosaurs and some large deposits of dinosaur bones have been uncovered, but there are far fewer kinds of dinosaurs than we have been led to believe. Dinosaurs designated as different types in many instances may just be variations within a "kind" — such as those we see within the dog "kind."

It is quite a distinction for a scientist to find the remains of a dinosaur, thus earning the right to give it a name. Maybe that's why when a set of bones is discovered that is similar to a pre-viously discovered set of bones, the newly-discovered set of bones is given a different name, especially when the bones are found in a different country or in a different part of the country.

Did You Know That Some Dinosaurs May Have Been Warm-Blooded?

The theory that some dinosaurs may have been warm-blooded has been around for some years. Though there is a great deal of convincing evidence to support it, it is not generally accepted. Why not? Because it destroys the evolutionary myth of "the age of the reptiles," during which time, mammals supposedly had not yet evolved. Mammals are considered to be much more intelligent than dinosaurs were, and supposedly at the time of the dinosaurs, intelligence had not yet evolved to the level of the mammals'.

Warm-bloodedness is normally associated with mammals and birds, so a warm-blooded reptile seems to be a contradiction in terms. According to evolutionists, birds and mammals are more advanced forms of life than dinosaurs. So for them to admit that the great flying reptiles such as the Pterosaurs and other creatures from the time of the dinosaurs may have been mammals would do away with the idea of an age of reptiles, which they have proclaimed as fact. Interestingly, fossilized remains of Pterosaurs have been found with imprints of fur. Fur or hair is a distinguishing mark of mammals.

Evolutionists are so persistent about the age of reptiles that they tag the early "dawn mammals" (mammals believed to have evolved first) found along with dinosaur skeletons, "mammal-like reptiles," not reptile-like mammals. One dinosaur skeleton that was found had a fossil of a mammal inside its stomach. Apparently, the mammal was lunch for the hungry dinosaur just before the dinosaur itself suddenly died.[2]

If it is true that some of the creatures previously thought to be dinosaurs were birds and mammals and not reptiles at all, then the so-called "age of reptiles" is nonsense. If birds, reptiles and mammals were all living at the same time, this is excellent scientific evidence in favor of Creation Science, which proclaims that all the birds, reptiles, mammals and other kinds of creatures were created all at once during days five and six of the creation week.

Scientists no longer believe dinosaurs were merely overgrown lizards. Paleontologists (scientists who study extinct forms of life through fossils) now believe they were special animals and cannot be stereotyped according to reptiles, birds, or mammals. Some were probably much faster, smarter and caring than has been previously thought — and much different than Hollywood's portrayal of them. Dinosaurs were unique, and must be viewed as such.

Did You Know That There Were Dinosaur Herds? (See fig. #33.)

A remarkable "bone bed" measuring two-and-a-half miles long and a quarter mile wide has been discovered. It contains an estimated 53 million dinosaur bones, all broken and jumbled together.[3] This evidence suggests there was a time when dinosaurs existed en masse — like the present-day great herds of animals still observable in Africa.

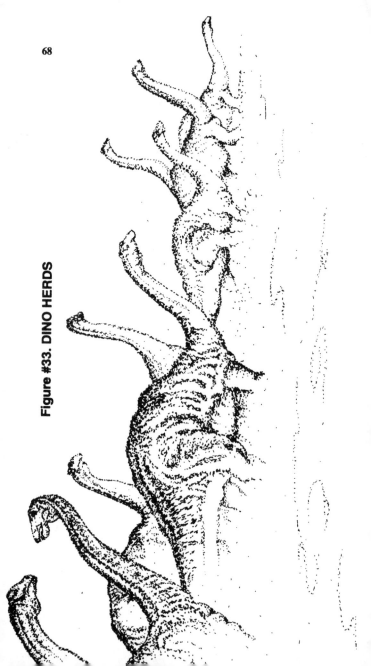

Figure #33. DINO HERDS

Chapter Four

How to Visit Temples of Evolutionism

Places to See Dinosaur Exhibits.

1. Alberta, Canada: The prehistoric park at the Calgary Zoo (There is also the Tyrell Museum nearby on dinosaurs located in Drumheller.)
2. Chicago: Field Museum of Natural History
3. Washington D.C.: Smithsonian Museum of Natural History
4. New York City: American Museum of Natural History
5. Jensen, Utah: Dinosaur National Monument
6. Los Angeles, California: Los Angeles County Museum of Natural History

Warning: Pagan Temples Dedicated to Ancestral Worship. (See fig. #34.)

On the continent of Asia and in the Far East,

Figure #34. ANCESTRAL WORSHIP

one can visit pagan temples and mosques dedicated to the gods of Buddha, Krishna and Allah. All of these temples are dedicated to the religions of man. In the West, there are also great temples that attract pilgrims by the thousands from all over the world. These also are dedicated to a religion of man: evolutionism. **(See fig. #35.)** These temples are called museums of natural history, but in reality, they are museums of evolutionary mythology. They are dedicated to man's religion unto himself, and his self-centered attempt to ascend into the heavens. Evolutionism is a religion that worships everything from the amoeba to man. **(See fig. #36.)**

These museums are superbly restored specimens of creatures that by and large died in Noah's Flood. But they are totally dedicated to the pagan mythology of the 20th century — evolutionism — the adherents of which are hostile to the idea of a special creation by God.

All the information about the creatures therein comes from an evolutionary viewpoint — one which totally discredits the concept of biblical creation and a supernatural God.

How to Make Pagan Museums Count for Creation Science.

Just as it is possible for a believer to gain

Figure #35. PAGAN MUSEUMS

Figure #36. AMOEBA TO MAN

insight by visiting a pagan temple of worship in Asia, so can visiting a museum dedicated to evolutionism be enlightening. And just as inoculations protect us from being harmed by encounters with bacteria, so can touring the man-made temples built to worship Western man's religions of humanism serve as protection against potentially harmful encounters with evolutionism.

There are several simple things one can do when visiting an evolutionary museum.

1. Look for displays (not models) that confirm creation or evolutionism. Example:

    a. The Bible in Genesis 1 states that all creatures reproduce after their own kind. Ducks produce ducks, dogs — dogs, etc. This is creation.

    b. Are there any displays of creatures (not models) evolving into another creature, revealing features that are only half formed? This is evolutionism.

2. When you see an exhibit that is dated (example: 100 million years), see what the evidence is for determining the age given. Is the age confirmed? If so, how? Or is the age only conjecture? Keep in mind that no one was around 100 million years ago.

3. Which exhibits testify to a Designer and

Creator and which testify to random chance?

    a.   Show children that in fact there is no evidence in the museum for evolutionism, but that all creatures testify to an intelligent Designer and Creator.

4. Is there any indication in the museum that recognizes a Creator? Or is the museum totally dedicated to humanism and to man's knowledge?

5. Which pictures and displays are actually confirmed as fact or are they only conjecture?

6. Which displays testify to the Genesis Flood? Consider how fossils are formed — through rapid burial.

7. Consider the evidence of any display that attempts to explain how life was formed, and compare the evidence with the Word of God. See if there are any samples of the original atmosphere in which evolutionists claim life spontaneously began as a result of blind chance.

8. Ask the museum guide and staff questions such as, "If evolutionism were true and creatures evolve and develop new characteristics in their appearance, then why do creatures such as the cockroach and centi-

pede still look exactly the same as the fossilized ones that are supposed to be over
350 million years old?

9. Show how laws of science such as the second law of thermodynamics (the curse)
confirm the Bible and are solid evidences
against evolutionism. Evolutionism
teaches that life is continually improving
itself and becoming more and more complex and intelligent, whereas the evidence
reveals just the reverse. This harmonizes
with the second law of thermodynamics.

10. Search for any evidence that substantiates
evolutionism's claim that inanimate matter
became a living organism. Or does God's
Word make more sense than believing that
some unknown chemicals in the past were
involved in an unknown process that has yet
to be duplicated in the laboratory but somehow produced some life forms that somehow reproduced themselves in an unknown
atmospheric composition at some unknown
place and unknown time in a soup of chemicals that is still undetermined? When all is
said and done, evolutionism is a religion to
the unknown god.

These are just a few ideas a Christian can use
when visiting a museum dedicated to evolution-

ism to show how the evidence is in favor of creation and against evolutionism. Remember, Christians are the salt of the world. Don't be afraid to take a Bible and read verses that counter evolutionism at each of the displays. Maybe someone nearby will be listening and will be challenged to consider the evidences. God has called us to be a light in a dark world.

The replicas of creatures from the dinosaur kingdom show us that dinosaurs did exist at one time, and some were highly unusual and very large. How unusual and how large is our next topic of discussion?

Chapter Five

Dinosaur Dimensions

(See figs. #37A & B)

Group Photos.

Because more and more well-preserved and complete dinosaur fossils are being found, scientists are gaining additional information as to what dinosaurs looked like. It is now known they came in all sizes; some were the size of a cat or dog **(see fig. #38)**, some weighed 100 tons or more.

Many of the dinosaurs were small — the size of children or even house pets. These dinosaurs were called the lightweights **(see fig. #39)**. Many walked on only two legs. There were horned dinosaurs **(see fig. #40)**, plated dinosaurs **(see fig. #41)**, and armored dinosaurs **(see fig. #42)**. There were those that had heads shaped somewhat like ducks; they are known as Duckbill dinosaurs. Some had bony heads and some horny heads. Others had bony crests on the top of their heads. These bony structures were hollow and

Figure #37A. DINOSAUR LINEUP

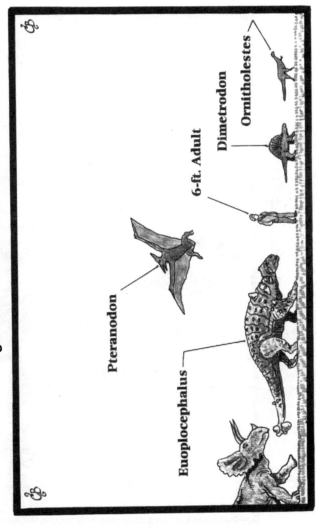

Figure #37B. DINOSAUR LINEUP

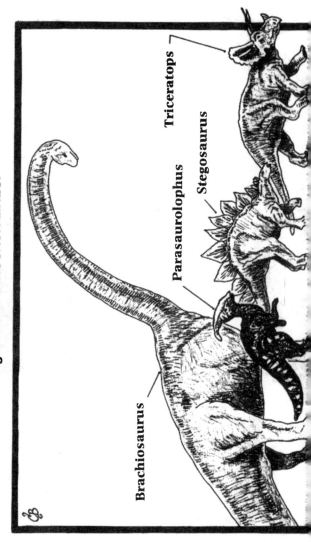

Brachiosaurus

Parasaurolophus

Stegosaurus

Triceratops

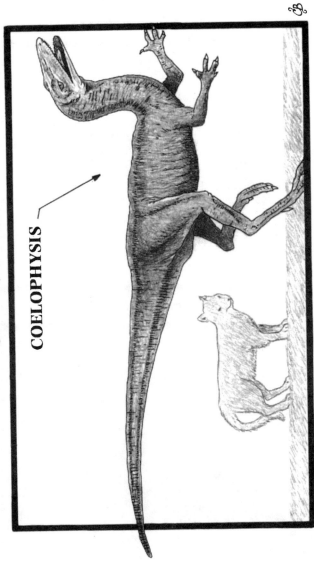

Figure #38. HOUSE PETS

COELOPHYSIS

Figure #39. LIGHTWEIGHTS

Figure #40. HORNED

Figure #41. PLATED

Figure #42. ARMORED

were connected to their nostrils by tubes (**see fig. #43**). There were huge vegetarians (**see fig. #44**), such as the Ultrasaurus that weighed 100-150 tons and needed huge amounts of food each day. The Ultrasaurus' daily food requirements were between four and five tons. There were also meat eaters (**see fig. #45**), some with terrible dagger-like teeth and claws shaped like switchblade sickles (**see fig. #46**). There were the "big birds" — flying reptiles whose beaks were full of teeth (**see fig. #47**), and marine reptilian denizens of the deep (**see fig. #48**).

Many people have only a mild curiosity regarding dinosaurs and fall prey to the media's depiction of them as always being gigantic monsters. Perhaps this is due to the fact that people have always had a fascination for the fantastic. While some of the dinosaurs were extraordinarily large, most did not exceed 30 feet in length, including their long tails.

The following descriptions will illustrate the unusual and peculiar makeup of the members of the dinosaur kingdom and may indicate another reason there is such a fascination with these creatures.

Dinosaur Gallery.

Can you imagine taking a ride through a

Figure #43. DUCKBILL

Figure #44. VEGGIE EATERS

Figure #45. MEAT EATERS

Figure #46. SWTICHBLADES

Figure #47. FLYING

Figure #48. MARINE

drive-through zoo that only had dinosaurs? Well, here are some of the creatures you might see — if dinosaurs were not extinct.

Scolosaurus (sko-luh-sawr-us). (See fig. #49.)

- An invincible "living tank"
- Size: Up to 18 feet long and 8 feet across at the midsection
- Covered with spike-studded armor, with knobs that stuck out 4 to 6 inches
- Had bony, knobbed tail wielding two spikes to ward off unwelcome antagonists

Figure #49. SCOLOSAURUS

Triceratops (try-sair-uh-tops). (See fig. #50.)

- Name meaning: "three-spiked head"
- Length: Up to 25 feet (about as long as a large delivery truck)
- Height: 10 feet
- Weight: Up to 24,000 pounds
- Had a head about 8 feet long

Figure #50. TRICERATOPS

- Had two massive horns over the eyes 40 inches long and almost a foot wide at the base

Hadrosaurus (had-ro-sawr-us).
(See fig. #51.)
- Height: 20 feet
- Length: 30 feet
- Rows of Teeth: 60
- Number of Teeth: 2,000

Stegosaurus (stegg-uh-sawr-us).
(See fig. #52.)
- Length: Up to 25 feet
- Famous for its "second brain" located along the spine above the hips
- Huge armor plates along its spine
- Height: Up to 12 feet high at the rear legs
- Curiously built, with low front legs and head
- Low to the ground
- Weight: Up to 20,000 pounds
- Note: The unique plates running along stegosaurus' backs are not found on any other dinosaur or reptile. If they evolved during millions of years of time as evolutionists say, we ought to have a series of transitional forms. But we don't have a single such intermediate form.

Figure #51. HADROSAURUS

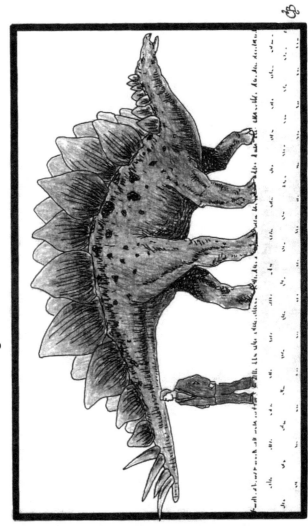

Figure #52. STEGOSAURUS

Euoplocephalus (YOO-oh-pluh-SEF-uh-lus). (See fig. #53.)

- Name meaning: True-plated head
- Length: 18 feet
- Weight: 2 tons
- Had a finer suit of armor than any medieval knight — even its eyelids were armor-plated
- Could topple and disable a T-rex with one well-aimed blow with its 3-foot-wide tail

Deinonychus (dye-NON-i-kus). (See fig. #54.)

- Nickname: Terrible Claw — because of its deadly curved claw like a cycle on its foot
- Possibly very speedy and warm-blooded, both of which characteristics are contrary to traditional evolutionary views
- Weight: 150 pounds

Baryonyx (BAYR-ee-ON-icks). (See fig. #55.)

- Nickname: Claws
- Recently found in England
- Had a snout like a crocodile
- Caught fish easily with its harpoon-like claws and 32 saw-like teeth.
- Length: 32 feet (equivalent of two automobiles)

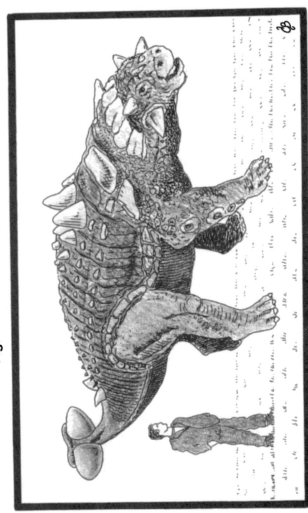

Figure #53. EUOPLOCEPHALUS

Figure #54. DEINONYCHUS

Figure #55. BARYONYX

Figure #56. SPINOSAURUS

- Weight: 2 tons

Spinosaurus (SPYE-nuh-SAW-rus). (See fig. #56.)

- Had an unusual sail on its back taller than a man, which may have been used to control body temperature
- Weight: 7 tons
- Length: 40 feet

Chapter Six

The Big Boys

Apatosaurus (uh-PAT-uh-SAW-rus).
(See fig. #57.)

- Length: 70 feet
- Weight: 30 tons
- Took the esteemed place of Brontosaurus as it was determined they were blood brothers
- Long head and tail served to help balance its body somewhat (like a tightrope walker who uses a long pole to help maintain his balance)
- A gentle giant (unless it accidentally stepped on you)

Diplodocus (dip-lahd-oh-kuss).
(See fig. #58.)

- Length: 100 feet (equal to 10 large elephants)
- Weight: 25 tons
- Had a second brain in its tail

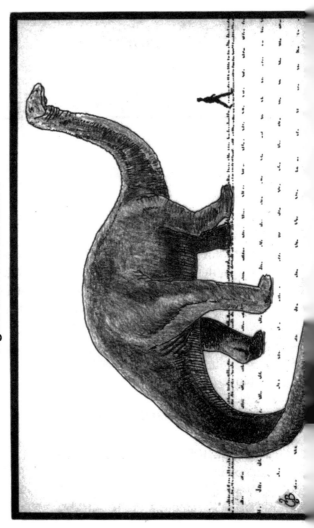

Figure #57. APATOSAURUS

Figure #58. DIPLODOCUS

- Quite harmless

Tyrannosaurus (tie-ran-uh-sawr-us). (See fig. #59.)

- Name meaning: king tyrant lizard
- Length: Up to 50 feet long (or as long as a railroad boxcar)
- Height: Up to 18 feet
- Weight: Up to 20,000 pounds
- Skull length: Over 4 feet
- Claws on hind feet up to 8 inches in length
- Teeth-like daggers — up to 6 inches in length
- Perhaps the fiercest of all the dinosaurs

Brachiosaurus (brack-ee-o-sor-us). (See fig. #60.)

- Height: 40 feet
- Length: 75 feet
- Weight: 180,000 pounds
- Daily food requirement: several hundred pounds
- Footprint as big as a bathtub

Supersaurus (soop-er-sor-us).

- Length: 80-100 feet
- Height: 50 feet at shoulders, with 20 additional feet of neck and head

Figure #59. TYRANNOSAURUS

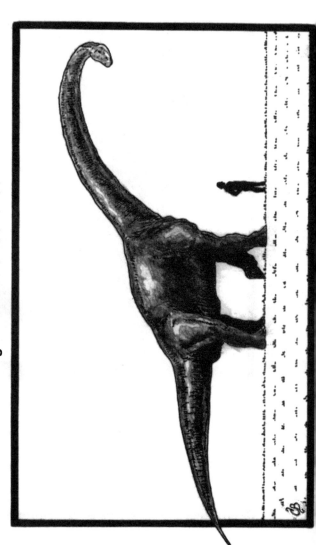

Figure #60. BRACHIOSAURUS

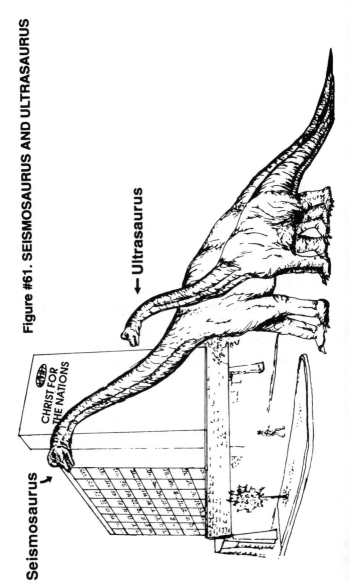

Figure #61. SEISMOSAURUS AND ULTRASAURUS

Seismosaurus

Ultrasaurus

- Weight: 60-70 tons

Ultrasaurus (ul-tra-sor-us). (See fig. #61.)

- Weight: 100 tons
- Length: Over 100 feet
- Height: At least six stories
- Required several tons of food a day.
- Discovered in 1979

Seismosaurus (siz-mo-sor-us). (See fig. #61.)

- Largest known dinosaur
- Name meaning: earth shaker
- Found near Albuquerque, New Mexico, in 1986
- Larger than two other recently discovered super-giant dinosaurs — Supersaurus and Ultrasaurus[4]
- Vertebrae resemble those of the Supersaurus from Colorado, but are 20 percent bigger
- Length: 120-140 feet
- Height: 60 feet high at the shoulder, with another 20 feet of neck and head
- Weight: 150 tons (a large elephant weighs only $7\frac{1}{2}$ tons)

Chapter Seven

Dinosaurs That Never Were

Non-Dinosaurs' Popular Misconceptions.

The following are reptilian-like creatures that are not considered dinosaurs, but which lived in the past. Some, like the Plesiosaurus, may still be living today.

Glyptodon (Glip-tuh-don). (See fig. #62.)

- Length: 15 feet (as big as a rhinoceros)
- Not a reptile, but a giant mammal of the past resembling an armadillo
- Had a bony outer casing like a series of

Figure #62. GLYPTODON

overlapping scale rings, enabling it to bend its body
- Had spikes on the knob-end of its tail that made it look especially suited for battle against any creature daring enough to try to get close

Dimetrodon (die-mee-tro-don).
(See fig. #63.)
- Had unusual sail-like fin
- Length: Up to 11 feet
- Weight: Over 650 pounds

Figure #63. DIMETRODON

Plesiosaurus (plee-see-o-sor-us).
(See fig. #64.)
- Length: 55 feet
- A water dinosaur
- Long neck was one of its distinguishing

characteristics
- May still be in existence today

Figure #64. PLESIOSAURUS

Pterodactyl (the-ro-dak-till). (See fig. #65.)

- A lizard-bird
- Wingspan: 35 feet
- Weight: About 50 pounds

Figure #65. PTERODACTYL

Pteranodon (tare-an-o-don).

Figure #66. PTERANODON

- Wingspan: over 50 feet (same as an F-4 fighter jet) and larger than a two-seater plane

Figure #67. SIZING UP THE BIG BIRDS

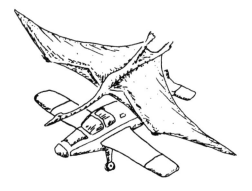

- Weight: About 400 pounds
- Had a 3-foot-long toothless beak
- One of the largest flying creatures that ever existed
- Fossil found in Texas

The Mammoth.

Figure #68. MAMMOTH

In addition to the dinosaurs, other creatures that are now extinct have been found. The woolly mammoth and the mastodon were somewhat like the buffalo or bison of North America. Actually, more fossils of extinct mammoths have been found than of dinosaurs. They were not as big as some dinosaurs, but they were bigger than elephants. They grew to 14 feet tall, and had tusks 13 feet long. In Job 39:9-12, a creature is described. That same creature is mentioned in Deuteronomy 33:17 as having horns. Some commentators call this creature a wild ox, others a unicorn, but the unicorn was probably a mythical creature. The description better fits that of the mammoth — a big bull with two horns. Mammoth fossils have been found in California, along with those of saber-toothed tigers. **(See fig. #69.)** The reason these huge creatures are now extinct may be that the bigger creatures lived longer millenniums ago.

If it were true what evolutionists claim — that everything is getting bigger and better — living creatures shouldn't be getting smaller and weaker, as they are. But the fossil record indicates that huge creatures that once roamed the Earth no longer exist, and that today's animals are smaller than they once were, and many have become extinct.

Figure #69. SABER-TOOTHED TIGER

Chapter Eight

"Bigfoot" and Big Lizards

Giants of the Past.

The size of the dinosaurs might not seem so strange to us if we realized the world once knew giant plants, giant insects **(see fig. #70)**, giant beavers as large as today's pigs **(see fig. #71)**, giant pigs as big as today's cows, **(see fig. #72)** giant sloths weighing ten thousand pounds, bears 20 feet tall, ostriches as large as giraffes, turtles with shells 10-12 feet in diameter **(see fig. #73)**, and giant rhinos that grew to over 17 feet tall **(see fig. #74)**. There is even evidence of giant human beings. Huge human tracks in stone, and enor-

Figure #70. GIANT INSECTS

Figure #71. GIANT BEAVER

6-ft. Man   Giant Beaver   Today's Hog

Figure #72. GIANT PIG

Today's Cow   Giant Hog   6-ft. Man

mous human skeletons have been discovered in various parts of the world.

Bigfoot.

Although a few people living today are over seven feet tall, and occasionally there may be someone as tall as eight feet, these heights are not normal in these times. But it may have been common for humans to be much taller before the Flood. According to the Bible, giants have existed since the beginning of man. There are

Figure #73. GIANT TURTLE

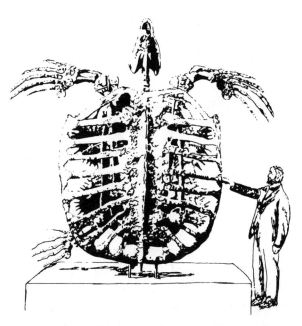

many written records of individuals in excess of eight feet. Besides Genesis 6:4 (KJV), there are additional references in the Bible describing giants, and even whole tribes or nations of giants. Since man's life span then was more than ten times that of modern man, it may be true he was also significantly larger in stature.

The most well-known example of a giant in Scripture is in the account of David and Goliath.

Figure #74. GIANT RHINO

Depending on the length of a cubit (17.5-20.65 inches), Goliath's height was $9\frac{1}{2}$ to 13 feet. Another giant mentioned in Scripture, King Og, was even larger than Goliath. King Og had a bed over 14 feet long. Adam, who lived nearly 1,000 years, may have been one of the tallest men ever.

Even today, there are vestiges of giants still living who provide us with a perception as to the immense size of such humans. Mohammed Allum Tena of Pakistan, presently the world's tallest man, stands 8 feet 3 inches tall and wears shoes nearly 2 feet in length.

Instead of being weird and unusual, giant reptiles were apparently common during the long life spans of early Bible days. In fact, the huge size of some of the dinosaurs may indicate great age since most reptiles, unlike mammals, continue to grow until they die. Dinosaurs enjoying longevity of life would harmonize with the biblical data (Gen. 5:1).

How Tall Was Adam?

Could it be that God created man much larger than we suppose? Some creationists have speculated that if we proceed backward in time to the creation, we might find man to be considerably larger than modern man. If modern man averages around 6 feet in height, Goliath was about 10 feet tall, and King Og was nearly 14 feet tall, could Noah have been even taller than 14 feet in height? And is it possible that Adam, the first man, could have been as tall as 16 feet? **(See fig. #75)**. If this theory is correct, the giant fossils of animals and dinosaurs appearing so extremely large to us today would not have had quite the same awesome, imposing and frightful effect on the ancients since they, too, would have been of enormous proportions. **(See fig. #76.)**[5]

Figure #75. GIANTS OF THE PAST

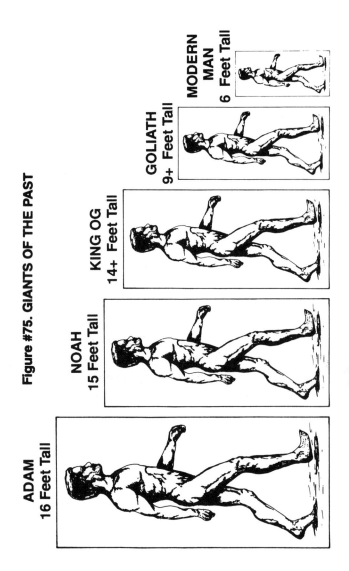

Figure #76. NOT SO BIG AFTER ALL

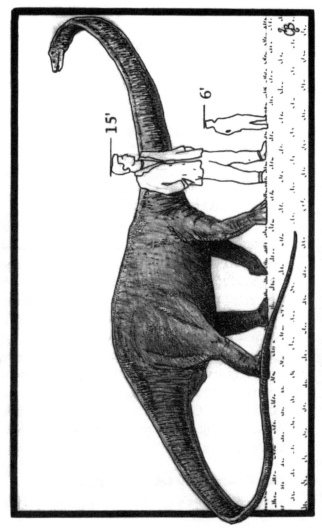

Chapter Nine

Why Did God Create Dinosaurs?

Many Mysteries Still Exist.

Everything God created was for a purpose. As Scripture reveals, God doesn't do anything without reason; otherwise, He could not be trusted. No one knows for sure what was in the mind of God when He created the dinosaur family. There are many creatures, such as the Australian platypus, which are presently living whose physical makeup and purpose **(see fig. #77)** are a mystery. It is even more perplexing to try to find the reason why God created these giant and strange creatures of the past that we call dinosaurs. One thing we can be sure of is that God created the dinosaurs to help maintain a balance within nature.

Dino Design: Marvels of Engineering.

The dinosaurs were marvelous examples of a

Figure #77. PLATYPUS

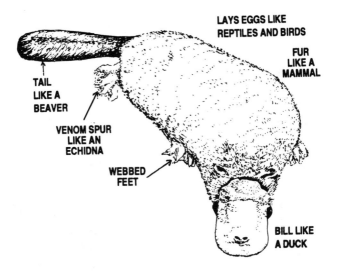

LAYS EGGS LIKE
REPTILES AND BIRDS

FUR
LIKE A
MAMMAL

TAIL
LIKE A
BEAVER

VENOM SPUR
LIKE AN
ECHIDNA

WEBBED
FEET

BILL LIKE
A DUCK

genius at work. Each dinosaur had to be engineered in a special way so that the frame could support its massive weight — more than 100 tons. These giant creatures of the past, such as Diplodocus, had limbs which were like supporting piers. The body below its spine was like a suspension bridge roadway held up by cables — much like the famous Golden Gate Bridge over the harbor of San Francisco, California. **(See fig. #78.)** Remember, it is one thing to design a 100-ton creature to swim in the ocean, like a whale, but it is an entirely different matter to

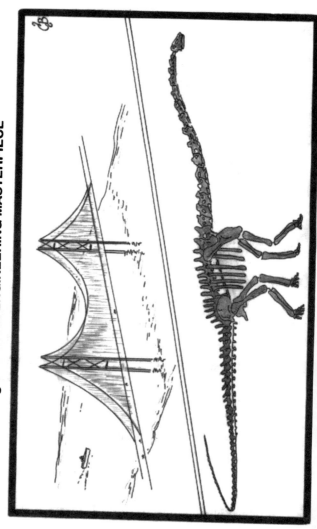

Figure #78. AN ENGINEERING MASTERPIECE

design a 100-ton creature that has to live, walk, climb and even run on land.

Think about the circulatory system that would be necessary to pump blood throughout the entire body of a giant dinosaur. Can you imagine the blood pressure it would take to pump blood up the neck of a Brachiosaurus some five to 10 stories above where its feet are planted on the ground? **(See fig. #79.)**

If dinosaurs were not engineered just right, even lowering and raising their heads would produce a walloping case of dizziness, much like we humans experience when we suddenly stand up after being in a reclining position. And can you imagine what it would feel like if your head went from ground level up to 50 feet in three seconds? These giant creatures were truly engineering marvels, and a great testimony to God's great power and wisdom.

In Volume IV of the Creation Series, *The Canopy Theory: World That Was*, an examination of the pre-Flood world reveals that at one time, the entire world was like a tropical forest. Massive amounts of foliage and gigantic plant life grew year round for 1,600 years — until the great Flood of Noah's day came and destroyed that world. Maybe the dinosaur population was created to serve as living lawn mowers to thin

Figure #79. TOWERING GIANTS

out the heavy foliage, thus providing an opportunity for smaller plants to grow among the
larger ones.

Now that evidence has been produced that
proves these giant creatures are fact rather than
fiction, what does the Bible have to say? In the
following chapters, the evidence for these creatures in the light of Scripture will be compared
with the "darkness" of evolutionism.

Chapter Ten

Dinosaur Origins

Looking Inside the Evolutionary Camp
(See fig. #80.)

Two Camps.

When it comes to the origin of the dinosaurs, there are two camps: the biblical view and the atheistic evolutionary view. Since atheistic evolutionists refuse to accept the idea of a Creator God, they conjured up a naturalistic, materialistic explanation for the origins of the universe and for the extinction of dinosaurs and other creatures. Unfortunately, there are even some Christians who have become divided on these issues.

The Evolutionary Camp.

The evolutionary theory presupposes dinosaurs evolved into existence some 200 million years ago (give or take 30 or so million). Then, for some mysterious reason, they became extinct about 65 million years ago. This is pure speculation based on a hypothetical theory of dating

Figure #80. TWO CAMPS

based on numerous assumptions with absolutely no solid evidence to validate it.

Evolutionists have devised a chart showing their statement of faith. The chart reveals their belief in time, and how time somehow brought about the development of plant and animal life. It systematizes everything by geological divisions of time. Evolutionists have named most of these periods of time after a person who discovered a rock strata or a place where a rock strata was first studied. The chart is hypothetical, and the rock stratum exists nowhere in the world in its entirety, except in the evolutionists' textbooks. **(See fig. #81.)**

When a scientist uncovers the bones of a dinosaur, he does not find a label indicating how old the bones are — no driver's license, no birth or death certificate, just bones. The idea that the bones are millions of years old is nothing more than a story evolutionists made up about the past. Keep in mind that no scientist was there to record when the dinosaur lived or when it died.

For many years some Christian theologians have attempted to accommodate the evolutionary time scale, because they naively believed the evolutionists' claims for their theory has been backed up with well-established facts. But on the contrary, evolutionism is not based on fact. It is

Figure #81. MYTHOLOGICAL CHART OF TIME

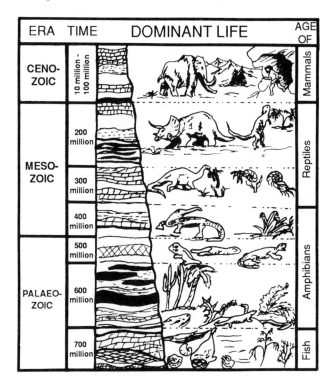

ERA	TIME	DOMINANT LIFE	AGE OF
CENO-ZOIC	10 million - 100 million		Mammals
MESO-ZOIC	200 million / 300 million / 400 million		Reptiles
PALAEO-ZOIC	500 million / 600 million / 700 million		Amphibians / Fish

merely a hypothesis, which is one step below a theory. It is supported only by the incredible faith of its advocates. Upon examination, it becomes obvious that the foundation upon which the hypothesis is based is very shaky. The evolution-ists have built a huge temple in which to worship their god of humanism; the foundation, however, is made of something more fragile than shiny tinfoil — vain imaginations (see Rom. 1:21).

The truth of the matter, we must realize, isn't about whether or not the evidences support evolutionism. The real issue is the evolutionists' desire to remove God and His Word from the picture. By doing so, evolutionists are left to write their own rules, thus directing their own destiny without any fear of eternal punishment for breaking the law of God. With God out of the picture, man can live according to his own standard of morality.

Chapter Eleven

The Evolutionary Mythological Dragons of the Past

Where Are the Transitional Forms?
(See figs. #82A & B.)

Probably one of the strongest cases against the theory of evolutionism is the fossil evidence itself. If evolutionism were true, there would be fossils of the intermediate forms — the various in-between formation stages of dinosaurs and other creatures.

Evolutionism claims that dinosaurs evolved over millions of years. If this were so, each creature slowly became another one. For instance, we are told that the amphibian slowly changed into the reptilian dinosaur. If this were true, there should be millions of transitional forms. Yet these transitional creatures have never been found, for they do not exist. If dinosaurs did in fact evolve from amphibians, there should be

Figure #82A. SOME TRANSITIONAL QUACKS

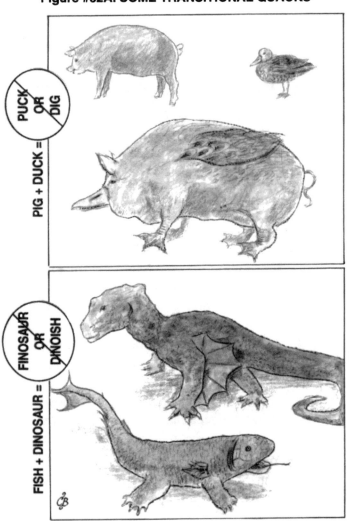

Figure #82B. SOME TRANSITIONAL QUACKS

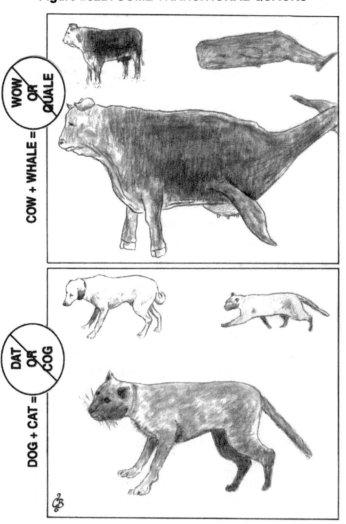

creatures in the fossil record that are half amphibian and half dinosaur. Yet there are no such creatures. If you visit any museum around the world, you will only see fossils of dinosaurs that are 100 percent dinosaur, never something in between. There are no creatures that are 25, 50, 75 or even 99 percent dinosaurs. They are 100 percent dinosaur or they are not considered a dinosaur at all.

What About the Strange Apparatus?

If evolutionism were true, there should also be fossil evidence showing the in-between stages in the formation of dinosaurs' unusual features such as the spikes and plates on the Stegosaurus and the strange-shaped skull of the Pachycephalosaurs. **(See figs. #83A & B.)** The armored dinosaurs that have spikes, horns and plates running along their backs and heads should have ancestors with spikes, horns and plates that are only partially developed. **(See fig. #84.)** Oh, the illustrations of intermediate forms in evolutionary books are quite impressive; but the museums contain only hypothetical illustrations and models because there is absolutely no evidence for them.

There are thousands of fossils discovered every year, and yet there is just no evidence of

Figure #83A. TRANSITIONAL FORMS: PLEASE COME FORTH

Figure #83B. TRANSITIONAL FORMS:
PLEASE COME FORTH

Figure #84. THE MISSING STAGES IN THE FOSSIL RECORD: ONE AND TWO

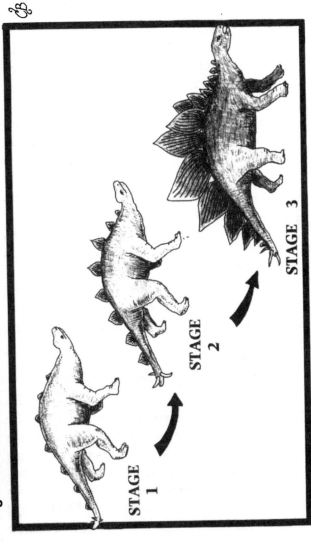

STAGE 1

STAGE 2

STAGE 3

developing intermediate creatures.

The distinctive features of certain dinosaurs appear fully formed in the fossil record of certain dinosaurs — no other creatures have even a semblance of such a feature. In other words, there are no intermediate forms. Why not? Simply because intermediate forms never existed. All creatures, including dinosaurs, were created by God — fully developed and fully functional with all of their unique characteristics. This is exactly what the fossil record reveals. With over 200 million fossils having been discovered so far, not one transitional form has been found. In fact, back in Charles Darwin's day, he admitted that the lack of intermediate forms was a strong objection to evolutionism.[6] However, he believed that in time they would be found. Well, have they?

Testimony From a Noted Evolutionist.

The noted senior paleontologist at the British Museum of Natural History in London, Dr. Colin Patterson, was asked why he didn't put a single picture of an intermediate form or a connecting link in his book on evolutionism, since his collection in the London museum houses over seven million fossils. He responded that if he knew of one, he would have put it in his book. In fact, he went on to assert, "I will lay it on the line, there is not one such fossil of which one might make a water tight argument." In another statement, Dr. Patterson declares that evolutionists are prone "to make up stories of how one form gave rise to another, and to find reasons why the stages should be favored by natural selection. But such stories are not part of science, for there is no way of putting them to the test."[7]

Oil companies have drilled wells throughout the world, examining layers of the Earth to depths in excess of five miles. They have come across many fossils, but no transitional forms. In fact, of the millions of fossils on Earth, not even one transitional form has been discovered.

The evidence reveals a planned and designed creation by a marvelous Creator. The fossil record reveals that every creature has remained what it was right from the very beginning, and this is what one would expect if he believes in the biblical account of creation.

Chapter Twelve

Inside the Christian Camp: "B" Band — Pre-Adamic Gapists

Two Bands.

Have you ever heard of "A" bands and "B" bands? The "A" band is comprised of the more knowledgeable and experienced musicians, while the "B" band has the less skilled and practiced, who are likely to occasionally bungle as they endeavor to play the right note.

In the Christian community, especially when it comes to the scientific, there are also "A" bands and "B" bands. We might compare the "B" band with Christians from earlier in the century. When they were confronted with the evolutionist's declaration that their theory was provable by using certain dating methods on fossils, they sought to find some way to make evolutionism and the Bible compatible. They came up with their own "song" — the gap theory, which makes room between Genesis 1:1 and 1:2 for a pre-Adamic creation that came and went between those two little verses. That way, they could counter the evolutionary stance — that the dinosaurs died out millions of years ago, and that there were once ape-like people roaming the Earth — with the idea that these were all a part of the pre-Adamic creation. But being that they were a "B" band, the "song" they came up with had some really sour notes in it.

For much of this century, the word "dinosaur" has been somewhat of an enigma, a stumbling block to many Christians who have been unable to see how dinosaurs fit into the traditional view of biblical creation. Some dinosaurs, with their tremendous size and huge proportions, are hard to visualize as having been created along with the other animals during the six-day creation week. As a result, Christians divided into two camps — the gapists and the creationists.

"B" Band: Pre-Adamic Gapists.

Let's take a closer look at the gap theory. For many decades and even today, many Christians have tried to ascribe dinosaurs to a pre-Adamic creation — one that took place before the six-day creation. They were bamboozled by the evolu-

Figure #85. THE GAP THEORY

FIRST CREATION GEN. 1:1	FALL OF SATAN ISA. 14:12	DESTRUCTION OF FIRST CREATION GEN. 1:2

BILLIONS
OF
YEARS

GAP

SECOND CREATION GEN. 1:3-31	TODAY	FUTURE JUDG-MENT I Pet. 3:11

DAY

2	3	4	5	6
Water and Sky	Land and Vegetation	Luminaries	Fish and Birds	Beast and Man

6000 YEARS

THEORY

tionists statements that they had scientific evidence for their theory. So many Christians have taken to the notion that there were two creations — the dinosaur creation, and the Adam and Eve creation. **(See fig. #85.)** Various passages of the Bible have been misinterpreted and mistranslated to accommodate this idea which presupposes that there was a gap of time between Genesis 1:1 and 1:2.

> In the beginning God created the heavens and the earth. And the earth was formless and void, and darkness was over the surface of the deep; and the Spirit of God was moving over the surface of the waters (Gen. 1:1,2 NAS).

The gap theory was concocted by Christians in an attempt to accommodate both the biblical creation and the evolutionary theory. It conveniently provides the time the evolutionists demand for the "geological ages." They came up with the idea that the millions of years in which the dinosaurs supposedly lived, a great cataclysmic event occurred, destroying these creatures and leaving the Earth "without form and void" (Gen. 1:2 NKJV). However, the geological ages are based on the principle of "evolutionary uniformitarianism" — a slow and gradual process which does not consider the possibility of a worldwide catastrophic flood. The "gap theory" is incorrect, being unwarranted biblically and impossible scientifically.

Well-meaning Christians who thought evolutionism and its geological ages were true, mistranslated various words in the Bible to try to accommodate the evolutionary theory. For instance, the word "was" in Genesis 1:2 was translated "became" and used to support the theory. Correctly translated, Genesis 1:2 should read "*was* without form and void," simply meaning empty, formless or unstructured, but not chaotic — a result of a catastrophe.

God created in steps. He first proceeded to "form" that which was "without form," then provided inhabitants for that which was "void." Another mistranslation involved Genesis 1:28 in which God supposedly commanded Adam and Eve to "refill" the Earth. "Refill" has since been corrected in most translations to read "fill."[8]

The fossil record reveals death, decay and destruction in Earth's history. **(See fig. #86.)** Romans 5:12 indicates there was no death in the animal kingdom until Adam sinned, which nullifies the possibility of a biblical concept of a pre-Adamic creation.

Figure #86. A TESTIMONY TO DEATH AND DECAY

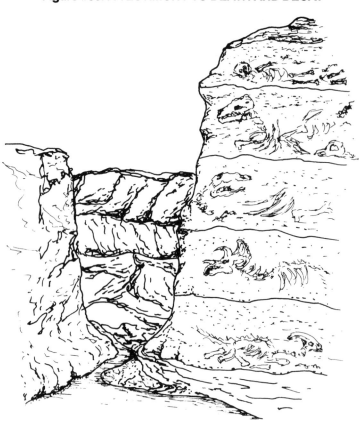

How can believers harmonize the gap theory
— a concept of a billion years of struggle for
existence, extinctions without number, disease,
confusion, disorder, decay, slaughter and death

— with a God of perfect wisdom, order, power, and grace, Who could easily have created all things complete and perfect from the beginning? How could a Christian, knowing the character of God, ascribe to the gap theory which teaches He chose the tortuous route of evolutionism? This is a serious theological problem that leads to a dead end. And how could God have said "it is good" after He finished His creation, if the Earth was full of the remains of death, decay and chaotic destruction?

The gap theory is simply not a viable one. Thus, the death and fossilization of dinosaurs must have occurred after the curse of Genesis 3.

Now the "A" band is playing loud and strong. Those who are numbered as members of the "A" band know that God's Word is true, and that tampering with it is dangerous. They are not afraid to confront the evolutionists about their ridiculous "proof." And they are finding that true science backs up the Word. The "B" band is still playing their "song," and some people are still listening. The reason is that they have not heard the symphonic melody — the heavenly song of truth that the "A" band is playing.

Chapter Thirteen

Inside the Christian Camp: "A" Band — Creationists

Creation Science View. (See fig. #87.)

On the other hand, the Bible clearly states that on the sixth day of creation, God made all the creatures of the land. In fact, during creation week, God made everything in the entire universe. Thus, man and dinosaurs lived at the same time (Ex. 20:11; Jn. 1:3; Gen. 1).

> And God said, "Let the earth bring forth every kind of animal — cattle and reptiles and wildlife of every kind." And so it was. God made all sorts of wild animals and cattle and reptiles. And God was pleased with what He had done (Gen. 1:24,25 LB).

Dinosaurs are reptiles. Remember, the word dinosaur was coined in the 1800s, and means

Figure #87. A LOOK AT THE SIX DAYS OF CREATION

DAY ONE:
And God said, "Let there be light." ... God called the light "day," and the darkness he called "night" (Gen. 1:3,5).

DAY TWO:
And God said, "Let there be an expanse between the waters to separate water from water." ... God called the expanse "sky" (Gen. 1:6,8).

DAY THREE:
And God said, "Let ... dry ground appear. ... Let the land produce vegetation" (Gen. 1:9,11).

DAY FOUR:
And God said, "Let there be lights in the expanse of the sky to separate the day from the night ... as signs to mark seasons and days and years" (Gen. 1:14).

DAY FIVE:
And God said, "Let the water teem with living creatures, and let birds fly above the earth" (Gen. 1:20).

DAY SIX:
And God said, "Let the land produce living creatures according to their kinds." ... Then God said, "Let us make man in our image" (Gen. 1:24.26).

terrible lizard. Genesis 1:21 refers to the creation of great sea creatures. The word translated "whales" in the King James Version is translated "great sea monsters" in most other versions. In other passages where this same Hebrew word, tanniym (tan-neem), occurs, it is translated dragon, monster, serpent or jackal (wild dog). *Strong's Concordance* says a tanniym is a "marine or land monster."

Dinosaurs were fossilized as a result of Noah's Flood, which covered the entire Earth. The Flood was the greatest disaster in Earth's history. All life was destroyed, then covered over by enormous mountains of mud, silt, sand and volcanic ash, entombing and fossilizing creatures of all sorts.[9] Of all the land creatures created, only the ones in the Ark were saved. They alone repopulated the Earth after the Flood. Dinosaurs were included in the repopulation, so Noah took them onto the Ark, no doubt very young ones that were still comparatively small. **(See fig. #88.)**

The Bible graphically describes a couple of creatures in the book of Job which perfectly fit the description of dinosaurs and dragons of the sea, as we shall examine in the following chapter.

Figure #88. ENTERING A BRAVE NEW WORLD

Chapter Fourteen

"Behold Behemoth"

(See fig. #89.)

Are Dinosaurs Mentioned in Scripture?

Although many Christians are not aware of it, there are creatures mentioned in the Bible that fit the description of dinosaurs. The actual word "dinosaur" is not mentioned because it is a modern term invented in the 19th century. In the book of Job, which is considered the oldest book of the Bible and is believed to have been written shortly after the Flood, there is a list of animals that includes two mighty creatures identified as behemoth and leviathan. God describes behemoth as the greatest of land animals. Its Hebrew name means "gigantic beast." The description of this creature in Scripture could easily match that of the large family of dinosaurs known as the Sauropods or grass-eating dinosaurs — two of which are known as Diplodocus or Apatosaurus. (See figs. #57 & 58.) Diplodocus had nostrils on top of its head so it could breathe with most of

Figure #89. BEHOLD BEHEMOTH: THREE PRIME SUSPECTS

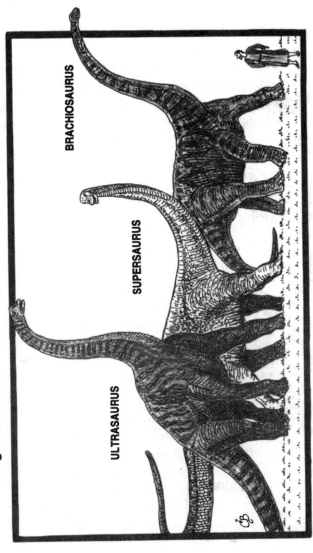

its head underwater.

The description of behemoth also fits closely the massive Brachiosaurus depicted by an artist in the book *Evolution* published by the Time-Life Association on Nature. Time-Life editors are not at all sympathetic to the creationists' position that man and dinosaur lived and existed at the same time. However, the sketch so resembles the words in Job that it is as if the artist were reading Job 40 as he painted his picture. **(See fig. #90.)**

Job 40: A Gigantic Beast.

> Look at the behemoth, which I made along with you and which feeds on grass like an ox. What strength he has in his loins, what power in the muscles of his belly! His tail sways like a cedar; the sinews of his thighs are close-knit. His bones are tubes of bronze, his limbs like rods of iron. He ranks first among the works of God, yet his Maker can approach him with his sword. The hills bring him their produce, and all the wild animals play nearby. Under the lotus plants he lies, hidden among the reeds in the marsh. The lotuses conceal him in their shadow; the poplars by the stream sur-

> round him. When the river rages, he is not alarmed; he is secure, though the Jordan should surge against his mouth. Can anyone capture him by the eyes, or trap him and pierce his nose? (Job 40:15-24).

This passage clearly indicates that creatures fitting the description of the reptilian dinosaurs lived in the Near East as late as 2000 B.C. during Job's lifetime; and remember, Job lived *after* Noah's Flood.

Scholars have labored to identify behemoth. Since the word means gigantic beast, commentators, thinking about the largest of animals living on the Earth today, have decided it must be an elephant, hippopotamus, or rhinoceros. The problem with that is, it doesn't fit the remaining verses portraying behemoth. In fact, no known living animal conforms to the characteristics listed in Job 40.

Consider the Following Detailed Description.
- It consumed the grasses.
- It had powerful muscles.
- It had bones like bronze.
- Its arms and legs were like beams of iron. **(See fig. #91.)**

Figure #90. RELAXING IN THE JORDAN RIVER

Figure #91. BONES OF IRON

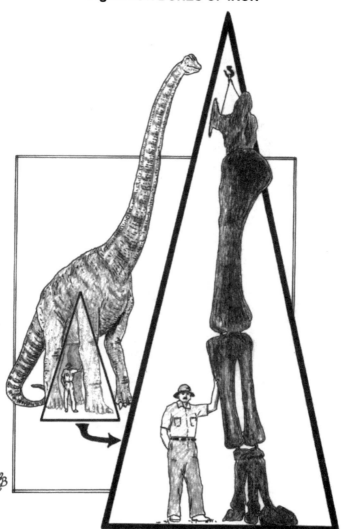

- Its tail was like that of a cedar tree.
- The roaring of a flooding river didn't alarm it.
- It couldn't be caught in a trap, let alone subdued and trained.
- It was "chief of the ways of God" — "ways" means biggest (Job 40:19 KJV).

The biggest dinosaur yet discovered was found in Alberta, Canada. Its bones show that it was found to be 150 feet long from its nose to the tip of its tail. **(See fig. #92.)** It is significant

Figure #92. 150 FEET LONG

that the word "marsh" is used in Job 40:21 ("fens" in KJV is the Hebrew word meaning swamp) because we know these giant creatures were comfortable on either land or in water.

The New American Standard Bible refers to this beast as a hippo in the marginal explanation. However, this is clearly contradicted by the reference to "his tail like a cedar" (vs. 17 KJV). Neither the tail of an elephant nor that of the hippo even vaguely resembles a tree **(see fig. #93)**: Their tails are more like a rope or a wet noodle than a cedar.

Figure #93. TRAILS OF TAILS

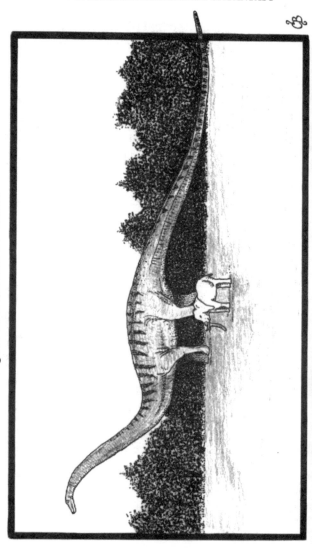

Furthermore, any circus will attest to the fact that elephants can be trained to do about anything, even roller skate, and that they are very friendly toward man. The creatures the Bible describes are not suitable.

The reason commentators are unable to identify this mighty animal is that they have apparently become extinct, although sightings of such creatures have been reported numerous times by inhabitants of remote parts of Africa. Unfortunately, modern Bible scholars for the most part, have become conditioned to think in terms of the long ages of evolutionary geology. So it never occurs to them that mankind actually lived in the same world with the massive animals found as fossils.

Since Noah's huge Ark could easily have held two of each known species of land animals, both living and extinct, dinosaurs were no doubt on the Ark, and afterward began to repopulate the world. Thus, Job and his contemporaries could easily have seen many kinds of animals which later became extinct due to the Earth's more harsh and demanding climate after the Flood, and the fact that the food resources were greatly diminished.

The behemoth was identified by God as "the chief of the ways of God" (Job 40:19 KJV), indicating it was the largest of all land animals. Inevitably, God was speaking of a mighty dinosaur. The description of behemoth does fit certain dinosaurs such as a Diplodocus or a Brachiosaurus, but does not fit any other creature known to man.

Creation Science advocates believe the dinosaur was created during creation week and lived and walked with man. But what does geology reveal?

Chapter Fifteen

Look to the Rocks, They Will Teach You (Job 12:8)

What Does Geology Say?

Scientific discovery confirms biblical revelation at this point.[10] Near the heart of Texas **(see fig. #94)** on the Paluxy riverbed outside the small town of Glen Rose, discoveries are constantly being made. Tourists visit the state park by the thousands every year to see the footprints of more than a dozen different types of dinosaurs embedded in the cretaceous limestone banks of the river.**(See fig. #95A & B.)** The finds include dinosaur footprints along with the footprints of humans. Not just one or two footprints — but dozens and dozens of human footprints in various locations, some even crossing the paths of dinosaurs. Occasionally, a human print is found *inside* a dinosaur print.

Numerous certified geologists have verified

Figure #94. DEEP IN THE HEART OF TEXAS

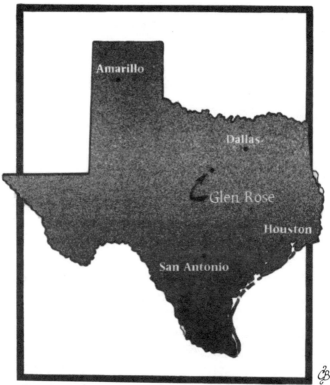

that the large "human prints" **(see fig. #96)** are genuine, as are the dinosaur prints; they were made within days, even hours, of each other. Genesis 6:4 tells us "there were giants in the earth" (KJV) at one time.

For years, reports have come out of Glen Rose

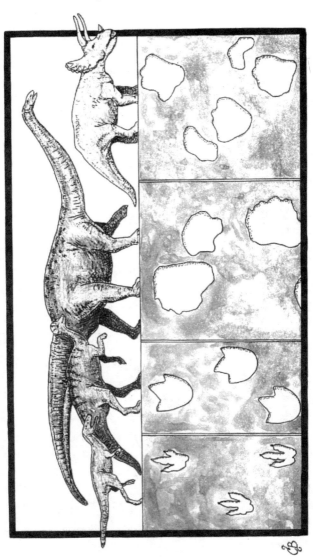

Figure #95A. BANK DEPOSITS ALONG THE PALUXY

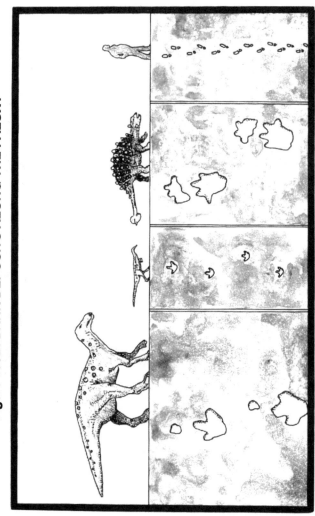

Figure #95B. BANK DEPOSITS ALONG THE PALUXY

Figure #96. HUMAN FOOTPRINT

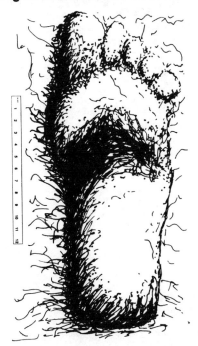

about "giant human footprints" among the dinosaur prints in the Paluxy River. **(See fig. #97.)**
These giant footprints seem to confirm this biblical statement. **(See fig. #98.)**[11] Since the rocks
often yield the bones of giant creatures several
times larger than their modern counterparts, why
couldn't the same be true with humans (see
Chapter Eight)?

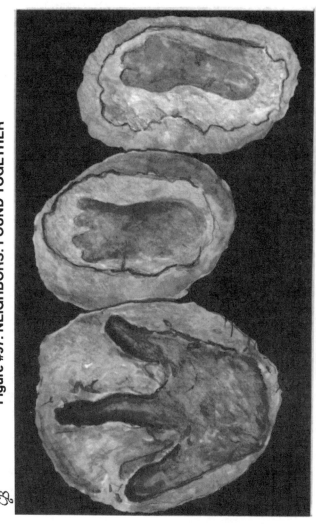

Figure #97. NEIGHBORS: FOUND TOGETHER

Figure #98. GIANT HUMAN FOOTPRINTS

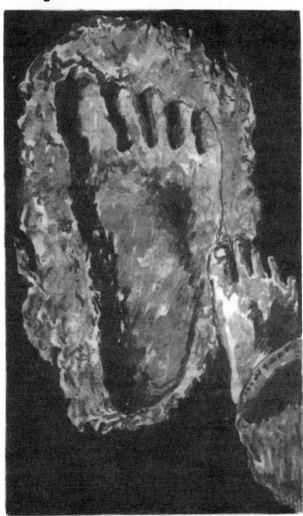

Chapter Sixteen

Dinosaurs: Deep in the Heart of Texas

Glen Rose, Texas: A Scientific Battlefield.

The findings at Glen Rose have attracted international attention, making it a scientific battlefield. At the Paluxy River near Glen Rose, there are numerous foot impressions with what has been interpreted by many creation scientists as the forms of the toe section, with a narrow arch, and a rounded heel of the human foot. The human footprints found in the riverbed (**see fig. #99**) come in three distinct sizes: 9, 15½, and 25½ inches. All were under limestone and about four inches of marl clay before becoming exposed through erosion. By evolutionary dating, the material is dated at 135 million years — some 132 to 134 (depending on the evolutionist) million years before man ever set foot on the Earth.

Figure #99. DINOSAUR STATE PARK

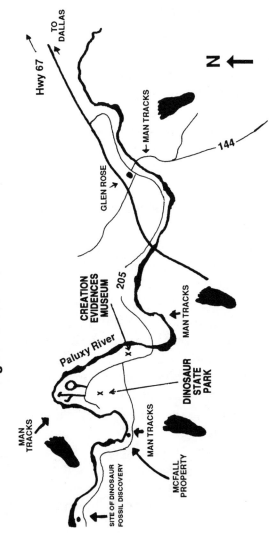

Statistics Keep Piling Up.

Around 200 dinosaur footprints, two major dinosaurs, and over 50 human-like tracks have been excavated. Creation scientists have excavated in the Paluxy riverbed:

- Five human prints, 25 inches each — indicating the man who made the prints stood over 10 feet tall.
- Thirty human prints, 16 inches each — suggesting the man who made them stood at least 8 feet tall and weighed as much as 400 pounds.
- Six cat prints, $7\frac{1}{2}$ inches across — signifying the creature was 6 feet at the shoulders and weighed 1,500 pounds.
- Trilobite, cat, man, and dinosaur prints have been found all on the same layer of strata. (These life forms represent an excellent cross section of the entire evolutionary [imaginary] column of time, from the beginning of life up to the present, supposedly consisting of 500 million years and more.)
- A dinosaur estimated to be 17 feet tall. (The entire rib cage and 14 feet of vertebrae have been uncovered.)
- One human footprint only 2 inches from a

dinosaur track, and six were in conjunction
with dinosaur tracks. (These tracks prove
that man and dinosaurs lived
simultaneously.)

Could They be Ape-Prints? (See fig. #100.)

Some skeptics have argued that a gorilla or an
orangutan might have made the prints, since they
also walk upright. Since according to evolution-

Figure #100. BIG TOE BALONEY

ism, neither gorillas nor orangutans existed until tens of millions of years after the last dinosaur became extinct, how could the evolutionists think the tracks could be theirs? Besides, these creatures have toes like fingers with a big toe **(see fig. #101)** like a human thumb on each of its four feet. **(See fig. #102.)**

Are the Impressions Genuine?

Some of the human footprints found on the Paluxy River have been excavated and sliced into segments to examine the surface below the print to determine if the print is a forgery. There are a number of points of interest that verify the genuineness of the human prints **(see fig. #103):**

- The impressions are normally exposed only by bulldozers or soil erosion.
- They are widely distributed in various locations.
- The rock particles found underneath the impressions are more compressed than the particles surrounding the prints, meaning they have not been carved by a forger.
- The mud up-push around the print, as the footprint displaced the layer into which they were forced, proves they are genuine.
- The sequence of prints, one footprint after the other, denotes they are authentic.

Figure #101. NOT EVEN CLOSE

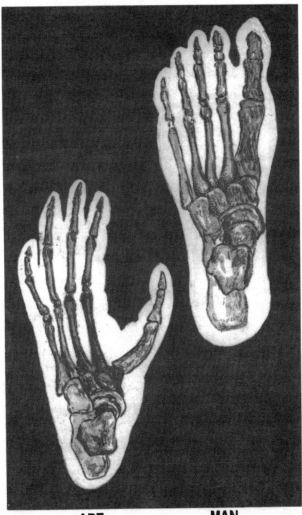

APE   MAN

Figure #102. IT'S AN APE. IT'S A YETI. IT'S A SASQUATCH. NO, IT'S A HUMANOID PRINT

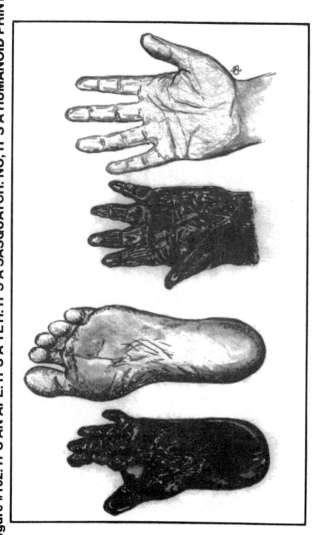

Figure #103. AUTHENTICITY OF HUMAN FOOTPRINT

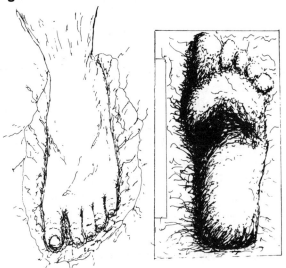

- The constant stride of a left-right, left-right pattern shows they are real.
- The size of the prints, as well as the stride distance, are constant.
- The barefoot human imprint is not like the imprint of any other creature. That it is human can be seen in the ball of the foot, the heel, the arch, the big toe, the toe line, and the toe depressions and ridges.

Eyewitness Reports.

Charlie Moss, a Glen Rose resident, found the first human tracks in the Paluxy riverbed in 1910.

Ernest Adams, an anthropologist, documented the existence of these tracks. Through the years, other footprints have been discovered by other residents of Glen Rose, such as Jim Ryals, Emmit McFall and his son, J.C. McFall, and many others. The human tracks were again verified in the 1940s by geologist Clifford Burdick, Ph.D. For years, Dr. Cecil Daugherty led tours so that people could see these human tracks firsthand. In recent years, other scholars have documented the tracks and substantiated their validity — Stan Taylor, Wilbur Fields, Mike Turnage, Fred Beierle, John Morris, Ph.D., Carl E. Baugh, Ph.D., and Clifford A. Wilson, Ph.D.

These people have impeccable credentials, and all have confirmed that the dinosaur tracks and the human footprints are side by side. This, of course, is revolutionary to the evolutionists. And it upsets their whole evolutionary geological chart — the one that exists nowhere except in the minds of the evolutionists and in the books they write.

How the Footprints Were Formed.
(See fig. #104.)

The footprints were no doubt formed in the early stages of Noah's Flood. As the tidal waters were coming and going, men and animals were

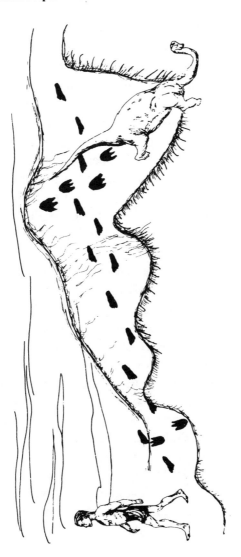

Figure #104. HOW FOOTPRINTS WERE FORMED

traversing the area, seeking higher ground. They left behind footprints in the soft mud which eventually semihardened, and were covered and preserved by additional layers of silt and mud. The kind of material of which the layers are comprised would have solidified within as little as 24 hours to the level of hardening that occurs with concrete. The many tracks indicate that the humans and the animals must have been racing for their lives, doing their utmost to escape the catastrophe about to engulf them. Gradually, the tides became more severe; the flood waters rose and all life was destroyed.

The soft limestone banks of the Paluxy River have been eroding, leaving footprints exposed in the stone. As time goes by, even the footprints erode and disappear. However, more prints keep appearing as the river continually cuts and erodes the rock. To accelerate the discovery of prints, creation scientists have been leading expeditions by utilizing teams of students and hydraulic equipment to remove rock to expose footprints of dinosaurs, other animals and man.

Attempts to Discredit.

Over the years, evolutionists have tried to dismiss these human fossil footprints as mere carvings or erosion markings. However, carved footprints are distinctly different in a number of ways, one being the characteristic of the step. Expeditions directed by creation scientists have offered evolutionary scientists, as well as reporters and other witnesses, the opportunity to watch as fossil tracks are uncovered. When several tons of limestone must be removed by a bulldozer and hydraulic jack to uncover prints, no one argues they were forged. A podiatrist (foot specialist) has confirmed the fossil footprints to be correct anatomically in every respect to human feet.

I Was a Personal Witness.

During the early 1980s, I had the privilege of witnessing several of the digs alongside the Paluxy River. I have personally seen numerous dinosaur and human footprints uncovered just inches away from each other.

The Press Was There.

On a couple of occasions, the press was on location with their cameras filming as teams physically removed a 12-inch layer of limestone. Weathered tracks led up to the edge, and it was believed they would continue under the limestone ledge, and they did. In 1982, both the press and many evolutionary scientists were invited to a dig. The press came in numbers, and their reports were somewhat favorable to the creation scientists' conclusions. In fact, the headlines of the *Fort Worth Star Telegram* (Thursday, June 17, 1982) read, "Tracks Step on Evolution."

The Evolutionists Dragged Their Feet.

Evolutionary scientists did not come until many months later, by which time the human tracks had been considerably enlarged because of their exposure to the atmosphere and to the eroding effects of the rain, wind and weather. Limestone begins a crumbling process as soon as it becomes exposed to the air, and it will dissolve when it comes in contact with rainwater. The limestone in which these tracks are preserved is very porous and therefore erodes quickly. Since it takes only about a week of exposure before a freshly excavated track (human or dinosaur) begins to weather in the soft limestone, tracks which have been weathering for several years are essentially worthless. (The fact that these tracks were so clearly preserved in this porous substance indicates rapid burial. Here again is evidence for the Flood.)

Arriving so long after the uncovering of the tracks, the evolutionists didn't have much to inspect at this site and thus were, as expected, quite skeptical. Evolutionary paleontologists do not challenge the dinosaur prints, but they do challenge the human prints. They insist dinosaurs and humans could not have walked together. According to their theory, cretaceous limestone hardened 120 to 140 million years ago, and the dinosaurs died out 65 million years ago.

No Faking It.

The fact is that those imprints were dug out with the press and many others watching. Casts were later made under video supervision; there was no possibility of "cheating" or faking those human footprints.

Chapter Seventeen

Footprints Discovered Inside the Iron Curtain

More Reports from Russia.

Glen Rose is not the only place human and dinosaur prints have been found together. Soon after the early 1980s excavations in Texas, reports came out of Russia that 1,500 dinosaur imprints had been found along with what appeared to be human imprints in the same strata. Several years before the collapse of the Soviet empire in Russia, newspapers[12] reported that thousands of dinosaur prints had been discovered on the Turkmenian Plateau. The article covered an expedition from the Institute of Geology of the Turkmen SSR Academy of Sciences, which found over 1,500 tracks left by dinosaurs.

The article also revealed that alongside the dinosaur tracts, bare human prints are visible. Now there are more than 3,000 footprints reported in the find. By evolutionary dating, the plateau is considered to be at least 200 million years old. Journalist Alexander Bushev reported that this discovery is very mysterious because according to evolutionism, humans appeared much later than dinosaurs. His explanation was that the prints must have been made by an extra-terrestrial. Coming closer to reality, some of the scientists suggested that man's history might need to be "extended."

According to Professor Amanniyazov, director of Turkmenia's Institute of Geology, "If further analysis proves that the prints have been left by anthropoids (man), the history of mankind will be extended to 150 million, not five million years." (Of course, from a creationist position there is no problem. We know that man and dinosaur lived at the same time, and apparently in close proximity to one another.) There were additional reports by journalist Alexander Bushev in *Komsomolskaya Pravda* (1/31/95), one of the leading popular newspapers of the former USSR, which confirmed the earlier reports.

Interestingly, this all took place before the collapse of the former Soviet Union, which means the commentary was an official report of the state. This is further substantiation that humans and dinosaurs did live together at one time in Earth's history.[13]

There Will Always be Infidels, Skeptics and Non-Believers.

There will always be a battle between the creation scientists and the evolutionists over the footprints. After all, the issue is not footprints; the issue is the existence of God. If the footprints are in fact human, then 150 million years of evolutionary history immediately bites the dust — not to mention the rest of the theory which would also be bankrupted.

Deception and Pride.

Why does man reject truth? Because he loves darkness more than he does light (the truth). As a result of man's rebellion against God, deception and pride set in.

> The coming of the lawless one will be in accordance with the work of Satan displayed in all kinds of counterfeit miracles, signs and wonders, and in every sort of evil that deceives those who are perishing. They perish because they refused to love the truth and so be saved. For this reason God sends them a powerful delusion so that

they will believe the lie and so that all will be condemned who have not believed the truth but have delighted in wickedness (II Thes. 2:9-12).

The sinner will continually look for a way by which he can escape God, His Word, His moral law, and the consequences of violating His moral law of love. It is amazing the lengths to which a person will go to dodge any threat of judgment so he can continue to do as he desires.

Chapter Eighteen

More Evidence Continues to Smother Evolutionism

Additional Discoveries.

In addition to the human tracks beside the dinosaur tracks, some fascinating objects have been found in the Paluxy River area that discredit the evolutionary myth.

1) A Human Tooth.

In June 1987, a fossil of a human tooth was uncovered in the Paluxy riverbed. The implications of this discovery are far-reaching. The tooth was found in cretaceous rock (dated by evolutionists to be 140 million years old) less than 30 feet from a fossilized dinosaur track, 56 feet from a fossilized human footprint, and 39 feet from a fragmented fossilized turtle bone. Several dentists and scientists have confirmed the tooth is a human incisor from a child between 4 and 8 years old. The tooth was found next to a dinosaur footprint in the same layer of stone.

2) A Trilobite. (See fig. #105.)

Figure #105. TRILOBITE

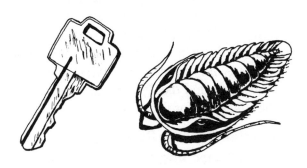

A trilobite fossil has been found in the same Glen Rose cretaceous rock layering. According to the evolutionary chart, the trilobite, a marine invertebrate organism, supposedly died out some 230 million years ago — over 100 million years earlier than evolutionary dates given for the Paluxy River limestone in which it was found. This discovery is exceedingly important, for it gives more evidence to support catastrophe, flood geology, and recent creation.

3) Saber-Toothed Tiger. (See fig. #69.)

Also found was another "out of place" fossil footprint. Saber-toothed tiger tracks were uncovered in this very same strata among all the other tracks. According to the evolutionary theory, at the time of the extinction of the dinosaurs, there were still only a few primitive mammals — nothing nearly so extravagant as a saber-toothed tiger, which supposedly didn't evolve until 30 million years later. To have tracks of this creature in strata of this age, and with dinosaurs whose footprints have been identified as the Brachiosaurus and the Tyrannosaurus, presents another dilemma for the evolutionist.

4) Iron Hammer. (See fig. #106.)

Figure #106. PRE-FLOOD ARTIFACT

There was another amazing discovery — an iron hammer embedded in rock. It was found 70 feet below the surface, predating man by millions of years according to evolutionism. The hammer was found near London, Texas, in rock dated by evolutionists at 435 million years. Evolutionists conjecture that this odervicion rock was forming when the first land creatures were evolving several hundred million years before man appeared.

There was no carbon in the hammer, which means it was formed differently than by the process of using coke or coal that has been used for the last 2,000 years, right up to the present day. There is no nickel in it, so it is not made of meteorite material.

This incredible discovery confirms the reality of Scripture: Man and dinosaurs were created together. According to the Bible, Tubel-Cain, only a few generations down from Adam, was a metalsmith "who forged all kinds of tools out of bronze and iron" (Gen. 4:22). Tubel-Cain and his offspring, to whom he no doubt passed on his trade, lived before the Flood. His descendants perished in the Flood; it is their tools which are being found in 20th-century excavations.

5) Panther Creek Woman.

The Panther Creek Woman is the name given

to a skeleton of a young woman found only about 12 miles, as the crow flies, from the Paluxy tracks by anthropologist "Bull" Adams. A 12-mile walk would have been easy for her since her skeleton reveals she was approximately seven feet tall.

6) Human Handprint.

In one place along the Paluxy River, the prints tell us that an individual slid in the mud and put his hand out to catch himself. The resulting footprints and handprint in the rock are consistent with the normal human position in such a situation. I had the privilege of placing my hand in the print, and it fit perfectly!

7) Dinosaur Fossil.

The remains of a dinosaur fossil were discovered by Dr. Baugh and his team in 1984 in the Paluxy River basin. This first dinosaur found in conjunction with dinosaur prints anywhere in the world counters evolutionary thought that dinosaur prints were made in marshy areas where fossilization could not occur because their remains would be scavenged and would decompose in such an environment. On the other hand, the find substantiates the view of creationists, who have long maintained that fossils are the result of a worldwide flood. This historic find involved a dinosaur that was caught in his tracks and buried under a tremendous deluge of water, clay and limestone.

8) Human Finger. (See fig. #107.)

Among the many remarkable discoveries, a fossilized finger identified as that of a human has also been found in the limestone strata of the Paluxy River.

9) More Footprints.

Some of the latest spectacular finds include 24 Tyrannosaurus footprints — with four human footprints among them. The human footprints are 16 inches from heel to toe. They, along with the dinosaur prints, were under 12 inches of solid limestone and four inches of marl. The prints are on the same limestone surface and are within inches of each other. The prints are in their original location; documentation shows there is no possibility of fabrication.

Figure #107. HUMAN FINGER

Chapter Nineteen

Evolutionary Desperadoes

An Evolutionary Counterattack.

As a result of the mounting evidence at the Texas excavations, evolutionists, in a desperate attempt to discredit the footprints, have come up with a counterattack. Now, after considerable study by even Bible-believing Christians, there is a warning being issued that *some* of the tracks may not be human tracks. Substantial caution is being advised by prominent Christian scholars who were previously supporters of the human track theory. It is said there is reason to believe that *some* of the "human-like tracks" show a three-toed dinosaurian feature, though it is indistinct in some of the prints. As yet, no assertions have been made as to what kind of creature made these imprints, but they are presently being examined to determine whether or not they are human. The tracks in question are six stone layers below and a quarter of a mile downstream from the Baugh excavations on the McFall property.

Whatever the outcome regarding this particular set of tracks, it will not rule out the possibility of humans and dinosaurs living on Earth at the same time. There are many other evidences that indicate they did. And keep in mind, the evolutionary geologic chart is only imaginary. The millions-of-years gap between man and the dinosaurs is not proven by facts. It is only 20th-century mythology.

What About Some of the Other Tracks?

Even though *some* of the mantracks have become controversial, the prints of animals found in the Paluxy River provide ample evidence to dispel the evolutionary theory. These other tracks affirm that trilobites, dinosaurs, woolly mammoths, bears, saber-toothed tigers, as well as humans, all lived at the same time. Their fossils and tracks have all been found in the same layer of strata.

How did these animals (which are supposedly late evolutionary developments) step back millions of years to the "time of the dinosaurs"? Isn't it much more logical that they lived together much more recently, like just prior to the great Flood as maintained in Scripture?

Additional Human and Dinosaur Prints.

Other petrified ancient human footprints have been found in a variety of places around the United States. Human footprints, both giant and normal size, have been found side by side with dinosaur tracks (Allosaurus, Tyrannosaurus or Brachiosaurus) in Arizona, Georgia, Missouri, Mexico, New Mexico, Kentucky and other locations in Texas.

Why the Battle?

If a person's worldview rests on evolutionary convictions, or if a person's job or position would be jeopardized by an admission that the evidence contradicts evolutionism, or if one believes everything uttered by well-known evolutionists is the absolute and unquestionable truth, then no matter what the truth of the matter really is, one will consider the creationists' view to be false.

When the first discoveries of the human-like footprints were made, there were scientists on location to study the prints — before erosion had made them what they are today. A number of those scientists were evolutionists, yet most of them affirmed that the tracks were indeed made by humans, or at least they admitted it was a strong possibility. This has been substantiated in documentary films and books.

Some biased evolutionists, who have not witnessed the uncovering of the tracks, have implied they are nothing more than water purposely smeared in the shape of a foot in an effort to make them appear like an impression. However, the evolutionists who first analyzed the footprints would have been able to feel whether there was actually an impression or whether foot-shaped designs were painted to trick people.

Evolutionists tend to pick at the gnats and swallow the bones. In one anti-creationist film, scoffers were shown sticking their feet into random and irregular holes in the rock, as if to say, "This hole must be a footprint, too." Snicker, chuckle!

The summarizing remarks in one evolutionary propaganda film say it all, "We figured before we came here that these were not human tracks." The reason evolutionists do not want to acknowledge that the tracks are human is because it would open the door to the truth of the Bible. This in turn would require admitting the existence of God, which is unthinkable to the unregenerate mind.

Final Analysis.

Though some say it may be improper for

creationists to continue to use the Paluxy foot-print data as evidence against evolutionism, there is still much that is not known about the tracks, and continued research is in order. Crea-tionists stand committed to truth, and will gladly modify or abandon any previous interpretation of the Paluxy data as the facts dictate.

A Possible Solution.

A possible solution to the dinosaur-shaped discolorations that appeared surrounding some of the impressions interpreted as human has been proposed by creation scientists Patton and Baugh: After the dinosaur tracks had been made in the lime mud (which later hardened into lime-stone), and had been filled in by a layer of similar but slightly chemically-different material that was able to later acquire a rust-colored discolora-tion through oxidation, a human traveled in the same direction. This human consciously chose to step in the partially-filled dinosaur tracks because doing so provided greater traction and stepping ease.

This proposed theory is consistent with the habits of humans walking or running in difficult areas. For example, double-stepping is the pre-ferred method for walking in snow. It is much easier to walk in the steps of another than to make a new path in fresh, soft snow.

The theory is supported by the existence of somewhat human-like impressions, each rather consistent in length, present inside the dinosaur tracks. The location of each impression is slightly different within each dinosaur track, and in several cases, human toe-like impressions are clearly visible in their proper form and configuration.

Although the theory is reasonable, it is only a theory. But the staining that has been so widely publicized is itself subject to questioning. Why have the stains suddenly appeared, and why are they associated both with tracks uncovered recently and with those uncovered many years ago? Experiments have revealed that similar stain markings can be produced quite easily with hydrochloric acid. It is not being suggested that the stains have been artificially produced, but that every possibility must be explored. It is also of interest to note that these markings, stains and splotches are found throughout the area where they were discovered and not just around the prints. Evolutionary critics, as always, have been very selective in their interpretations and their reports.

The interpretation of the tracks is subjective, meaning that one's interpretation will be based on one's overall worldview. If one's worldview is evolutionary, then the interpretation will be anti-creation. If one's worldview is based on Creation Science, then the interpretation will be in favor of the biblical concept.

Chapter Twenty

Tiny Creation Vessel Sinks Evolutionary Battleships

Creation Evidences Museum.

Dr. Carl Baugh, a prominent creation scientist who has done substantial research in the Paluxy River quest, has established the Creation Evidences Museum (located en route to Dinosaur State Park). In this small museum, there are more artifacts in favor of Creation Science than there are in favor of evolutionism in all the evolutionary museums throughout the world. There is enough evidence in favor of biblical creation to sink the entire evolutionary fleet of battleships. Among the artifacts presently on display at the museum are:

- Human footprints in stone (dated cretaceous — 140 million years old)
- Iron hammer in stone (dated Ordovician — 435 million years old)

- Giant cat print in stone (dated cretaceous)
- Moab man skeleton excavated from stone stratum
- Nebraska man tooth (used in Scopes' evolutionary trial)
- Trilobite in stone (dated cretaceous)
- Casts of recent footprint excavations
- Handprint in stone (dated cretaceous)
- Signed letters of verification from scholars

Creation Museum Address.

CREATION EVIDENCES MUSEUM
P.O. Box 309
Glen Rose, Texas 76043
Telephone: (817) 897-3200

The museum is located on Farm Market Road 205 near the Paluxy Bridge in Somerville County, Texas. **(See fig. #99.)**

Scopes' Trial Evidence. (See fig. #108.)

One of the museum's displays includes an original 1925 newspaper article on the Scopes' trial — which claimed as its two lines of evidence for evolutionism, the missing links, Piltdown man (a fossil hoax) and Nebraska man (concocted from a fossil pig's tooth).[14] **(See fig. #109.)** This exhibit clearly validates the fact that evolutionism is nothing more than a 20th-century myth.

Figure #108. NEBRASKA MAN: RESURRECTED FROM A TOOTH

Latest Discoveries.

Recently, more human-like fossil footprints have been discovered at the Paluxy River. The

Figure #109. AN EXTINCT PIG'S TOOTH

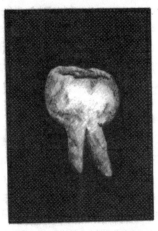

announcement of the new discoveries was made
by geologists from the Institute for Creation
Research (ICR). Three new human-like footprints were discovered by Dr. Carl Baugh and Dr.
Marlin Clark. This discovery followed others
made a few months earlier by Dr. Baugh and Dr.
John de Vilbiss. The newly discovered imprints
show some evidence of human toe marks and
other features which seem to point to their being
made by human feet. The prints show no evidence of the discolorations which appeared
around some of the other tracks, making them
appear reptile-like.

Dr. John Morris and Professor David

McQueen from ICR stated the new prints are still insufficient to convince skeptics, at least until the trail can be extended. Study of the source of discoloration surrounding some of the older prints is continuing at ICR. Results will be published later.

Carbon Dating.

It is also interesting to notice that with all its faults, carbon dating occasionally comes down on the side of the creationists' viewpoint as it has in the Paluxy River debate. Dr. John Morris has reported that carbon testing was applied to plant life found in the same layer of cretaceous limestone supposedly 140 million years old. The date given was approximately 800 years — a long way from 140 million years.

Furthermore, the dinosaur bones found have been carbon dated and found to be only 39,000 years old, which further substantiates the untrustworthiness of carbon dating as well as the imaginary nature of the immense ages assigned to the dinosaurs. The 65-million-year gap between the dinosaurs' extinction and man's arrival can only be considered a fictitious myth.

On Par With the Dead Sea Scrolls.

For Christians, the discoveries at Glen Rose,

Texas, are on par with the discovery of the famous Dead Sea Scrolls of Israel. **(See fig. #110.)** The Dead Sea Scrolls, discovered in 1947, substantiate the accuracy of the Old Testament, which had been attacked for centuries by atheistic skeptics. They mistakenly concluded that the Old Testament which we have today could not possibly be what was originally written, since several thousand years separated the original manuscript from the oldest copy in existence. The discovery of the Dead Sea Scrolls quickly silenced the skeptics, revealing once again God's ability to preserve His Word. The fact that there is very little difference in the text is a tribute to the great care taken by the copyists. It gives fresh grounds for confidence in the reliable transmission of God's Word down through the centuries.

Likewise, the discoveries at Glen Rose and the Paluxy River are a continual threat to the evolutionary myth; and thus are vehemently attacked by skeptics.

Figure #110. DEAD SEA SCROLLS ON PAR
WITH PALUXY FOOTPRINTS

Chapter Twenty-One

Leviathan: Fire-Breathing Dragons

(See fig. #111.)

The first enormous creature mentioned in the book of Job is behemoth, as discussed earlier. The second one is leviathan. Is this creature symbolic and meant only to portray a truth, yet in reality never existed? Or could it be that such a creature actually roamed the Earth at one time?

Job 41.

1.   Can you pull in the leviathan with a fish-hook or tie down his tongue with a rope?
2.   Can you put a cord through his nose or pierce his jaw with a hook?
3.   Will he keep begging you for mercy? Will he speak to you with gentle words?
4.   Will he make an agreement with you for you to take him as your slave for life?
5.   Can you make a pet of him like a bird or put him on a leash for your girls?

Figure #111. LEVIATHAN

6. Will traders barter for him? Will they divide him up among the merchants?

7. Can you fill his hide with harpoons or his head with fishing spears?

8. If you lay a hand on him, you will remember the struggle and never do it again!

9. Any hope of subduing him is false; the mere sight of him is overpowering.

10. No one is fierce enough to rouse him. Who then is able to stand against me?

11. Who has a claim against me that I must pay? Everything under heaven belongs to me.

12. I will not fail to speak of his limbs, his strength and his graceful form.

13. Who can strip off his outer coat? Who would approach him with a bridle?

14. Who dares open the doors of his mouth, ringed about with his fearsome teeth?

15. His back has rows of shields tightly sealed together.

16. Each is so close to the next that no air can pass between.

17. They are joined fast to one another; they cling together and cannot be parted.

18. His snorting throws out flashes of light; his eyes are like the rays of dawn.

19. Firebrands stream from his mouth; sparks of fire shoot out.

20. Smoke pours from his nostrils as from a boiling pot over a fire of reeds.
21. His breath sets coals ablaze, and flames dart from his mouth.
22. Strength resides in his neck; dismay goes before him.
23. The folds of his flesh are tightly joined; they are firm and immovable.
24. His chest is hard as rock, hard as a lower millstone.
25. When he rises up, the mighty are terrified; they retreat before his thrashing.
26. The sword that reaches him has no effect, nor does the spear or the dart or the javelin.
27. Iron he treats like straw and bronze like rotten wood.
28. Arrows do not make him flee; slingstones are like chaff to him.
29. A club seems to him but a piece of straw; he laughs at the rattling of the lance.
30. His undersides are jagged potsherds, leaving a trail in the mud like a threshing sledge.
31. He makes the depths churn like a boiling caldron and stirs up the sea like a pot of ointment.
32. Behind him he leaves a glistening wake; one would think the deep had white hair.
33. Nothing on earth is his equal — a creature

without fear.
34. He looks down on all that are haughty; he
is king over all that are proud.

Was Leviathan a Crocodile? (See fig. #112.)

Historically, man has captured, killed, and made good use of the crocodile. Verses 6 and 7 rule out the possibility that the leviathan is a crocodile. In fact, crocodiles have been hunted so successfully, they are considered by some to be an endangered species.

Verses 26-30 describe methods which might be used to attempt to capture leviathan, and why they would be fruitless. In verse 30, leviathan is described as having armor plates protecting his underside, as well as his upper parts. A crocodile's underbelly is very soft and vulnerable.

Verse 9 indicates that the bravest of men would fall in fear *at the very sight of him* — hardly a fitting description of an encounter with a crocodile, which adults have ridden like a horse and wrestled in amusement parks. Verse 9 is supported by verse 25, which mentions leviathan's huge size, and its ability to raise itself high into the air. A crocodile can raise itself perhaps 12 inches, whereas a dinosaur could raise its head 20 to 40 feet — and some even higher.

Figure #112. CONSIDER CORKY THE CROCK

Not an Elephant, Rhino or Whale, Either. (See figs. #113A & B).

In various English translations, the animal is called "leviathan." In the original Hebrew, the word used is "livyathan" (liv-yaw-thawn) — great water animal (or great water serpent or large sea monster). A 19th-century engraving depicts a great water creature. Sightings of such monsters have been reported throughout history by sailors aboard seagoing vessels. **(See fig. #114.)**

The whale could certainly be considered a great water animal; but a whale is not impervious to capture by man, nor does it fit the description of leviathan. A close examination of Job 41:1 indicates that leviathan was an unusual type of animal — huge and ferocious, coated with armor and mail (closely-fitting scales), and with sharp projections around the belly and underneath. The fact that leviathan had mail (vs. 3) definitely rules out elephants, rhinos and whales, which are all mammals. This description does fit some types of dinosaurs, but does not at all fit the elephant, the crocodile or the whale.

"No one is fierce enough to rouse him" (vs. 10). And, "When he rises up, the mighty are terrified" (vs. 25). Verse 33 says, "Nothing on earth is his equal." Does this sound like a whale,

Figure #113A. OTHER POSSIBILITIES

Figure #113B. OTHER POSSIBILITIES

an elephant or a crocodile — all of which have
been fairly easily killed or captured by man since

Figure #114. MONSTERS OF THE SEA

long before Christ's time?

Sea Serpent?

The Hebrews had words for crocodiles, elephants and whales. Why would those words not be used in Job 41? This leviathan was something different. The biggest difference was breath. The smoke and fire (verses 19-21) indicate a huge, fierce animal with very powerful breath. **(See fig. #115.)**

This creature's breath was so powerful it could burn up its enemies. If God created a dinosaur that breathes fire, He can surely carry out the punishment He has planned for His enemies.

> God is just: He will pay back trouble to those who trouble you and give relief to you who are troubled, and to us as well. This will happen when the Lord Jesus is revealed from heaven in blazing fire with his powerful angels. He will punish those who do not know God and do not obey the gospel of our Lord Jesus (II Thes. 1:6-8).

> They marched across the breadth of the earth and surrounded the camp of God's people, the city he loves. But fire came down from heaven and

Figure #115. NO SMOKING. PLEASE

devoured them (Rev. 20:9).

William Beck's translation (and others) of verse 34 reads: "He looks down on all high things as a king over all proud creatures." This is a fitting description of an Allosaurus, Tyrannosaurus rex or a Stegosaurus. The fierce sea serpents Elasmosaurus and Tylosaurus **(see fig. #116)** can also be considered as candidates, though none of these sea creatures are known to have breathed fire. Some scholars have suggested that leviathan may mean the dinosaur family as a whole, not just one particular kind.

A Closer Look at the Fire and the Smoke.

Many commentators on the book of Job explain away the fire and smoke. They say that as the sea monster (leviathan) plowed through the water, the steam issuing from his nostrils resembled fire and smoke. They do not believe the leviathan actually exhaled fire and smoke. Yet the statements in these verses are very explicit, there can be no misunderstanding: The monster's breath kindles coal, and flames leap from its mouth. Thus we believe the clear statements in the book of Job prove such monsters did exist at some time in history, though there are no present-day observable dinosaurs or sea monsters which exhale fire and smoke.

Figure #116. ELASMOSAURUS AND
TYLOSAURUS

Legends of Fire-Breathing Dragons.

The stories of fire-breathing dragons from various locations on Earth have always been considered legends — nothing but a romanticized myth. But many legends are based on things which really did happen, although every detail in the story may not be true. It's hard to believe that the same story could have been invented by all those different people from around the world.

For example, the story of the Flood has been found in over 200 accounts, and among some peoples who could not have heard it from the Bible. All the details are not exactly the same as those in the biblical version; nevertheless, the numerous accounts of the Flood let us know there really must have been one. The many stories of dragons, therefore, indicate that these creatures really existed at one time.

Legendary Monsters.

The following are examples of fire-breathing creatures that have been reported throughout history, some even in recent times.

The Chimaera of Roman and Greek mythology, described as being half-horse and half-dragon, was said to breathe out fire and smoke.

In two books, *The Great Orm of Loch Ness*

(1969) by F.W. Holiday, and *In The Wake of the Sea-Serpents* (1968) by Bernard Huevelmans, the authors authenticate that in the past, large creatures did inhabit bodies of water. And, they report even now, there are huge creatures living in a number of the world's lakes and oceans, some of them capable of making an explosion.

In *The Celtic Dragon Myth* by George Henderson, a report is given on legends centering in the Highlands and Isles of Scotland. All are similar to legends told throughout the world, including the dragon of St. George, and a dragon in the area of Palestine which had breath so powerful, people dropped dead before getting within bow range. Henderson also mentions a legend from the Scottish Highlands regarding St. Gilbert and a fire-breathing dragon. A great dragon had set fire to magnificent forests in Ross, Sutherland, leaving them charred, blackened and half-decayed. His fiery breath made a desert of the land.

There is a dramatic poem by the German poet, Gottfried of Strassburg (A.D. 1210), titled "Tristan and Iseult," which takes place in Ireland. In the poem, the king promised his daughter, Princess Iseult, to the brave man who would slay the monster. Tristan went after the monster, and as he drew near, it spewed forth smoke and flame from its open jaws. Tristan threw his spear through its heart, but the powerful monster killed Tristan's horse, and his shield was burned to coal by the flame from its mouth. Finally, Tristan dug his sword into the monster's heart, and it expired with a roar so terrible it seemed heaven and Earth had collapsed.

The historical testimony, outside of Scripture, strongly suggests there may have been such creatures. Too, there is the scientific witness: We know of creatures living today which, on a large scale, would be similar to the descriptions of fire-breathing dragons found both in Scripture and secular history. One thing is certain, we cannot say such things are impossible.

Chapter Twenty-Two

Nature's Living Creatures of "Fire"

Nature's Unique Chemical-Producing Creatures.

But how could a creature generate fire? What kind of chemistry would it take to do that? To find a possible answer, let us consider a few amazing creatures that can give us clues.

Light Creatures of the Night: A Glowing Tale.

Figure #117. FRIENDLY FIREFLY

In 1967, while working with Youth With A Mission on the island of Dominica in the Caribbean Islands, I was able to read from my Bible one moonless night without using electric lights or my flashlight. A lightning bug made it possible for me to read an entire chapter without any difficulty. By squeezing off the tail of the insect, I was provided light for some time before it faded.

But how can this little creature produce light? It does so by manufacturing chemicals that produce a glow. Man has discovered how to duplicate this chemical phenomenon, and markets it to the public in the form of flashlights, plastic necklaces and other Fourth of July trinkets. When the chemicals mix, they give off a glow for several hours.

The flash on the lightning bug was designed by God for the purpose of courtship and mating. The light it creates is 90 percent energy efficient: It gets the most light for the least amount of effort to produce the light. The average household light bulb is only four percent efficient, with the remaining energy being converted to heat. Man has a distance to go to catch up with nature's intelligence — or should we say nature's Creator's intelligence.

Can you imagine a creature the size of an

elephant being capable of producing enough electricity to light up its entire body? It sounds impossible, but if the tiny lightening bug can do it, why couldn't it be done by a much larger creature? For years, Walt Disney World Electric Parade had man-made mechanical creatures — hippos, beetles, bears, pigs, horses and carriages, trains, ships, Looney Tunes characters, and even dragons that hissed smoke — which were totally illuminated by lights. It was quite amazing. Each electrical carriage received its power from chemicals in its batteries. What is even more amazing is that there are living creatures that produce electrical phenomena — and some can generate enough power to kill a human.

The Electric Eel. (See fig. #118.)

The rivers of South America are home to the electric eel. The eel has special organs in its body that work like batteries to produce electricity. It is capable of producing a shock of up to 650 volts, which is five times the strength of a common 110-volt household electrical outlet. An adult eel can kill a person on contact and stun a horse.

I have a video clip of an encounter between an alligator and an electric eel. The alligator was huge in comparison to the eel. The conflict was

Figure #118. A STUNNING REVELATION

over almost before it started. One shock sent the alligator into convulsions. It survived the ordeal, but was left stunned and virtually motionless.

Chapter Twenty-Three

A Beetle That Blasts Its Adversaries

(See fig. #119.)

Talk About Chemical Warfare!

One of the most fascinating natural chemical reactions is found in the bombardier beetle. It produces two kinds of chemicals and keeps them in two separate chambers until it is ready to mix

Figure #119. BOMBIE, THE BLITZING BEETLE

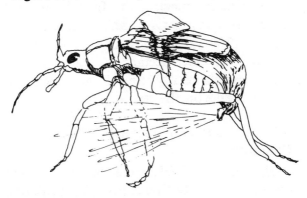

them. This beetle's defense system is a cross between tear gas and a tommy gun. When the beetle senses danger, it internally mixes enzymes contained in one body chamber with concentrated solutions confined to a second chamber. The combining of these rather harmless compounds, hydrogen peroxide and hydroquinones, generates a noxious spray of burning benzoquinones, which explodes from its body at a scalding 212 degrees F. It shoots out the mixture in rapid pulses before the chemicals can do any damage to it. Microscopic investigations reveal that the tiny creature can emit violent pulses of spray at an astonishing rate of 500 beats per second. If a tiny creature can do something this amazing, what do you think a giant beast might be able to do when on the attack?

Even more amazing, the fluid is pumped through twin rear nozzles, which can be rotated like a B-17 World War II Bomber's gun turret to hit, with bull's-eye accuracy, a hungry frog, a giant tarantula or a swarm of ants seeking to overpower the tiny beetle.

A Look at Bombies' Internal Combustion Chambers.

How could leviathan breathe out fire and smoke? Amazingly, God in His infinite wisdom, has created a miniature version of a fire-breathing dragon which fires gases from twin cannons. The bombardier beetle is only about half an inch long, but can produce what it takes to make an explosion within its body and then shoot it out against spiders, frogs, or any other creature seeking to devour it. The explosion is not powerful enough to burn the hand of a human because the beetle is so small. But it is real; and the beetle can direct this explosion with remarkable accuracy against predators.

Bombie's defense system detonates the evolutionary theory right into oblivion. How is it possible for such a system to have evolved by accident over thousands of years, which according to evolutionism would require thousands of genetic mistakes (mutations) in order for it to come to its present complex and sophisticated defense mechanisms? Think of the odds of it surviving. Just one mistake, just one wrong mutation, and the beetles' future is destroyed. Kaboom!! And he blows himself into beetle heaven. Why did the bombardier beetle not blow itself up in the development of its complicated machinery? It has to be able to manufacture just the right chemicals, keep them in two separate chambers until it is ready to use them, and be able to produce the enzymes that make it possible to fire off the chemicals quickly enough so it does not self-destruct. How incredibly complex! **(See fig. #120.)** This is powerful evidence in favor of creation.

Figure #120. INSIDE THE AMMO DUMP

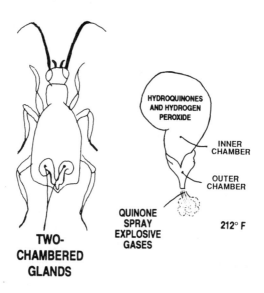

HYDROQUINONES AND HYDROGEN PEROXIDE

INNER CHAMBER

OUTER CHAMBER

QUINONE SPRAY EXPLOSIVE GASES

212° F

TWO-CHAMBERED GLANDS

If the bombardier beetle can do this amazing feat, then it is entirely possible dinosaurs breathed out fire and smoke. Neither the legendary Chinese dragon nor the creature leviathan, spoken of in Job, are beyond the bounds of possibility or reason.

Six Conditions for Making Fire.

For leviathan to have breathed out fire and smoke would require just six components: 1) oxygen, 2) controlled humidity, 3) friction, 4) sulphur, 5) phosphorous, and 6) a way of making an electric spark.

When leviathan lifted its neck out of the water, it would have had both oxygen and friction. Its scales were so closely joined together that no air could get in or out; thus it had controlled humidity. It could have made an electric spark in the same way as the firefly or the electric eel. The sulfur and phosphorous could have been produced internally.

Strange Apparatus on Fossilized Dinosaurs.

If the modern-day bombardier beetle is able to produce an explosion, isn't it possible that monsters of long ago had the capability of exhaling smoke and fire? There were numerous dinosaurs which spent a lot of time both in the water and on land.

Curious Heads.

The configurations in the skulls of some dinosaurs mystify anatomists. **(See fig. #20.)** Perhaps these mysterious cavities, which are comparable to the chambers found in the bombardier beetle, were part of a mechanism which gave them an ability to exhale fire and smoke. This would explain the universal legends which describe such fire-breathing creatures.

Artillery Skulls.

Pachycephalosaurus belonged to a group of dinosaurs which were nicknamed "boneheads." No one knows the purpose for the bumps on their necks, noses and heads.

The Parasaurolophus had strange chambers on top of its head and tubes connected to its nostrils. **(See fig. #121.)** It might have had a chemical apparatus similar to that of the bombardier beetle, but on a larger scale. The crest at the top of the skull of the Duckbill dinosaurs, Corythosaurus Casuarius, enclosed a complex system of air pouches and nasal passages, the function of which remains a mystery to paleontologists.

It is biologically possible for the legendary ancient fire-breathing dragons to have actually existed. These beasts could have accumulated enormous pockets of a flammable hydrocarbon such as methane. Methane, after all, is produced in the digestive system of bloated cattle and may have been likewise in dinosaurs. A bombardier beetle-like apparatus could have ignited the

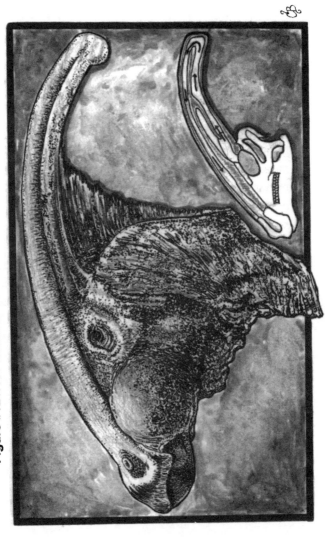

Figure #121. A PRIMARY CANDIDATE: PARASAUROLOPHUS

vapors belched forth from a frightened dinosaur, giving it the capacity to be a living flame-thrower. Yes, biologically it is possible. **(See fig. #122.)**

Who is King Today?

On the North American continent, there is one animal that is considered to be the king of the animals: the grizzly bear. It will not back down under any circumstances no matter who or what comes against it. The only exception is the skunk; Mr. Grizzly has learned that the cost to tangle with that small critter is too great.

The otherwise harmless and friendly Texas skunk **(see fig. #123)** ejects noxious chemicals to frighten off its would-be attackers. Change the chemicals to the flammable ones, add a few other parts and a spark, and you would have a not-so-harmless Texas critter.

Figure #122. DINO COMBAT

Figure #123. SKUNK ALERT

Chapter Twenty-Four

Spiritual Implications of Behemoth and Leviathan

Why So Much Space?

Behemoth and leviathan have more space devoted to them (44 verses) than the other 12 creatures mentioned in the book of Job combined. The characteristics described correspond to no known living animals. Why would God devote so much attention to these two fearsome animals in the concluding and climactic portion of His message to Job (and for His children to read down through the ages)?

> The LORD said to Job: "Will the one who contends with the Almighty correct him? Let him who accuses God answer him! ... Would you discredit my justice? Would you condemn me to justify yourself?" (Job 40:1,2,8).

It appears Job had set himself up as a judge of God's dealings with mankind. This prideful and arrogant attitude leads to deception. We can fall easily into the same satanic trap if we are not continually and consciously submissive to God's Word. In these verses, God was challenging Job's arrogance.

Pride is the same sin the devil exhibited, and the one for which he was judged. God must judge pride within us as well. God said to Job:

> Do you have an arm like God's, and can your voice thunder like his? Then adorn yourself with glory and splendor, and clothe yourself in honor and majesty. Unleash the fury of your wrath, look at every proud man and bring him low, look at every proud man and humble him, crush the wicked where they stand. Bury them all in the dust together; shroud their faces in the grave. Then I myself will admit to you that your own right hand can save you (Job 40:9-14).

Job was humiliated and speechless after this rebuke from God. He could no longer defend his own righteousness. He could only acknowledge his own corrupt and impure heart in the presence of his Creator God, and wait for Him to enlighten his blindness. God does so by using two of His creations, behemoth and leviathan.

The Message of Behemoth and Leviathan.

God's reference to behemoth was meant to emphasize His tremendous creative power, as this animal was far greater than any previously mentioned. Some of the dinosaurs were not only the largest, but also the most awesome and fearsome of all the animals God created. They must have induced terror in ancient man, which is why they probably became a symbol of evil, giving rise to the tales of dragons that have been passed down from the ancestors of almost every nation of the world.

Job's Pride.

Why did God confront Job with the characteristics of the fire-breathing creature called leviathan? Was God trying to get across to Job that some of his characteristics were like those of leviathan?

The powerful characteristics of leviathan represented Job's pridefulness. Leviathan's overlapping scales signified Job's invincibility. Nothing could break through and penetrate his heart. The fire was symbolic of Job's response to others with scorching words. There was a need for humility in Job's life. Though he was an extremely righteous man, close to God and a man of faith, he had not overcome his pride. God described behemoth and leviathan, the two gigantic dinosaurs, to show Job his pride. These enormous creatures were incapable of changing or humbling themselves. Job, too, was having a problem with changing. He needed a confrontation with God.

The Word says Job was the greatest man of the East (Job 1:3). God bragged about him again in Job 1:8 and 2:3; he feared God and refrained from evil. But the greatness God had given Job was threatened seriously because of Job's arrogance.

Like the behemoth, Job felt he could stand in the middle of the Jordan River (life) at flood stage (trouble), and it would not overthrow him. He had become puffed up with his strength, greatness and power. Like the behemoth, Job had escaped all the snares and pitfalls his friends had set up to try to capture him. But the blessings of God had gone to his head; because of his pride and stubbornness, Job was being taken to task by God Himself.

God Compares Job to the Unmanageable Leviathan.

In speaking of leviathan, God was comparing

Job to this unmanageable creature. Job had been breathing out fire and smoke, as leviathan did. His fiery breath was aimed at his friends which was wrong, even though they did treat him badly. He bragged about his righteousness. He accused God of being unfair with him, and demanded a legal confrontation with God.

Job declared in a bitter manner that God was against him, and was making him suffer for the sins of his youth (Job 13:26). He claimed God was responsible for putting his feet in stocks (Job 13:27). He asserted that God had delivered him to the ungodly, and turned him over into the hands of the wicked (Job 16:11). Job contended that God's army had surrounded him and were encamped against him (Job 19:12). He complained about the wicked not being punished for their sins in this life, questioning the providence of God (Job 21,24). He maintained that whether he went forward, backward, left or right, he could not find God (Job 23:8,9). He was so upset, he wanted to write out his grievances, and boldly bring them against God (Job 31:35).

Job, like leviathan, was strong, proud, powerful and arrogant. As God described this massive creature which breathed out fire and smoke, Job saw the resemblance between himself and leviathan; he realized how high and mighty he had been acting. This revelation brought him to his knees in repentance. God was then able to restore his health and bless him doubly.

The Pride of Mankind.

This arrogant attitude is prevalent in all mankind. Unless man humbles himself before the Almighty and accepts Christ as Lord and Savior, he will be destroyed by God's consuming fire. Evolutionism carries this arrogant spirit, for it was not born of man, but of Satan himself — the epitome of pride and arrogance.

The way of the believer must not be one of pride, arrogance, nor of personal retaliation against offenders. The way of the believer must be to follow in the footsteps of our Lord Jesus, Who did not defend His personal rights. The Bible says, "He was oppressed and afflicted, yet he did not open his mouth; he was led like a lamb to the slaughter, and as a sheep before her shearers is silent, so he did not open his mouth" (Isa. 53:7).

> Your attitude should be the same as that of Christ Jesus: Who, being in very nature God, did not consider equality with God something to be grasped, but made himself nothing,

taking the very nature of a servant,
being made in human likeness. And
being found in appearance as a man,
he humbled himself and became obedient to death — even death on a cross!
(Phil. 2:5-8).

Of Christ's obedience the Word says: "Therefore God exalted him to the highest place and
gave him the name that is above every name"
(Phil. 2:9). Our obedience will likewise be
rewarded.

Chapter Twenty-Five

Why Dinosaurs Didn't Sink Noah's Ark

(See fig. #124.)

How in the World?

Many creationists believe that Noah, in following the command of the Lord to save at least one pair of *every* kind, took dinosaurs aboard the Ark. **(See fig. #125.)** (Of course, the marine dinosaurs would not have required the safety of the Ark.) The question which comes to mind is, "How in the world did Noah get two of each of the huge dinosaurs on the Ark?"

Contrary to Public Opinion.

Dinosaurs came in a variety of sizes. Contrary to public opinion, not all of them were giants. Some that have been found frozen in stone were so small that their skulls could fit in a thimble. Keep in mind that although there have been numerous accounts of the supposed dinosaur genera (up to nearly 1,000 in some evolutionary

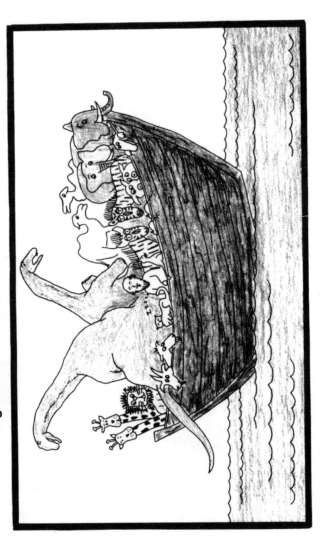

Figure #124. "ABANDON SHIP, ABANDON SHIP!"

Figure #125. HERE COME THE BIG BOYS

books), only about 100 weighed more than 10 tons when they were fully grown. In other words, only that many would have been about a third larger than the size of an African elephant.

Most of them were probably closely related — meaning the number the evolutionists promote is most likely far too high. Thirdly, the Bible nowhere states that God took fully-grown dinosaurs onto the Ark. No doubt the dinosaur family was represented by the young, not the adults.

Dinosaurs laid soft rubbery eggs, like reptiles do today. The largest dinosaur egg found thus far measured only about a foot in length, or about the size and shape of a football. **(See fig. #126.)**

This reveals that dinosaurs started out very small in size. So the pair of dinosaurs God chose to enter the Ark were rather small. **(See fig. #127.)** That way, the Ark could easily handle the weight of these inhabitants.

No doubt God selected a minimum number of dinosaurs, knowing which variety had the potential to produce different sizes, shapes and assortments — like the 200 plus different breeds of dogs in existence today. **(See fig. #128.)**

Some skeptics argue that all the breeds of dogs couldn't have come from only one pair of wild dogs. This theory discredits the need for

Figure #126. GRADE AAAAA EGGS

Figure #127. A FLOATING NURSERY

Figure #128. CHARTING CANINES

only a pair of each kind to be on the ark. A counter response would be, "Isn't this idea more realistic than the evolutionary notion that all the dogs originally came from a pair of rocks?" **(See fig. #129.)** Evolutionists believe life supposedly came from inanimate matter — rock.

Noah would not have had to take full-grown specimens onto the Ark; God most likely brought the young to Noah. Since many of the dinosaurs hatched from eggs no larger than a turkey egg **(see fig. #130)**, during the early part of their lives, they were very small and would have fit easily into the Ark. All animals outside the Ark, including dinosaurs, perished in the Flood.[15] **(See fig. #131.)**

Figure #129. CHARTING ROCKS

Figure #130. TINY TOTS

Figure #131. DOWNFALL OF THE DINOSAURS

Chapter Twenty-Six

What Become of the Dinosaurs That Survived on the Ark?

Have All Dinosaurs Died?

Although the fossil record reveals that billions of creatures died and were buried because of the Flood, what happened after the Flood to the dinosaurs that survived in the Ark? Where are they? There are thousands of creatures living today that are offspring of creatures that survived on the Ark. So where are the dinosaurs?

To answer the question, "Have all dinosaurs died?" we must remind ourselves of the definition of "dinosaur." As previously mentioned, dinosaur simply means "terrible lizard." If this is the correct meaning, then dinosaurs are not extinct. Reptilian lizards still exist: the iguanas of Central America, the Komodo dragons **(see fig. #132)** of South East Asia, not to mention the

Figure #132. DRAGONS OF KOMODO

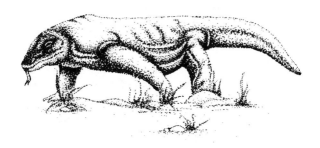

many reptiles with which we are familiar here in America, such as the alligator.

The Komodo Dragons.

About 1,000 huge dragon lizards still survive on the small Indonesian island of Komodo (see *National Geographic*, December 1968). We don't usually think of them as dinosaurs simply because evolutionism has wrongly taught us to think of dinosaurs as strange creatures from the past. But when the monitor lizard (Komodo dragon) was first found in the East Indies, it was reported to be a dinosaur. Scientists of the day rejected the reality of this creature, but today the monitor lizard is recognized as a living and dangerous carnivorous reptile. It reaches a length of seven feet, and is a powerful fighter, dangerous to man.

The American Alligator. (See fig. #112.)

Although they are now almost extinct and seldom exceed 12 feet in length, the American alligator attained lengths of nearly 20 feet as recently as the turn of the century (see *National Geographic*, January 1967). The marine crocodile, which is found off the northern coast of Australia, can, even today, exceed 30 feet. And notice these creatures are found in more tropical areas — like the pre-Flood Earth.

Changing Definitions to Save Face.

Although dinosaurs are reptiles, evolutionists are giving new meaning to the term "dinosaur." This helps them maintain a separation between the so-called the Dinosaur Age, and those reptiles which are somehow still living today. No doubt this is helping to save face in evolutionists' circles. It keeps them from having to explain why some reptiles survived and some did not. Scientists have decided that the major feature which distinguishes dinosaurs from other reptiles, such as crocodiles and alligators, is the position of their legs.

Dinosaurs had a fully erect posture much like an elephant, whereas other reptiles, such as the alligator, have limbs which sprawl out to the sides of its body. Dinosaurs walked much like the elephant whereas the alligator "waddles," so to speak, as its limbs project sideways from its body. Thus, they have placed those like the alligator and Komodo dragon in a different class. Nevertheless, they by and large are cold-blooded reptiles created by God on the sixth day along with all of the other reptiles, including those that lived in the so-called Dinosaur Age.

Reptile Growth.

An interesting and significant fact about reptiles is that they continue to grow in size and length for as long as they live. Mammals have secondary centers of ossification in the growing ends of their bones. When these centers have replaced most of the surrounding cartilage, they fuse with the bone shaft so that no further growth can take place. Most reptiles do not possess these secondary centers, so their bones are free to grow throughout life. If a reptile lives for 100 years, it will grow for 100 years. Increasing the life span of the iguana, Komodo dragon, alligator, turtle, and boa some 15 times would result in a very large reptile.

The Post-Flood World.

Because of the catastrophic nature of the worldwide Flood, the Earth was no longer the same afterward. It was no longer the lush, tropical place it had been before. The tropics were isolated to a small area, with much of the Earth cooler and more damp than before. This placed the dinosaurs that came off the Ark, particularly the large ones, at a distinct disadvantage.

In addition, Scripture tells us that life spans decreased significantly after the Flood. Most reptiles grow during their entire lifetime, but the post-Flood Earth did not allow dinosaurs, or any other creature, long lives. So the reptiles did not grow to the sizes they did before the Flood. The shorter life spans took away their advantage over the large mammals, who have growth limitations. Nevertheless, the dinosaurs from the Ark, and probably some of their descendants, did survive for a time, some for centuries. History is full of documented eyewitness reports of such.

Chapter Twenty-Seven

Historical Records of Dinosaurs

(See fig. #133.)

Dragon Folklore.

Since the Bible states that all creatures were created during the six days of creation, then dinosaurs had to be included at this time. With these giant creatures roaming the Earth during the history of man, there should be numerous stories of dinosaurs throughout the world from many nations. And in fact, this is exactly the case.

Historical accounts of dinosaurs are numerous since the time of the Flood. Again, it must be noted that all civilizations have accounts of dragons and large beasts in their legends and myths. However, since the term "dinosaur" was not invented until the 19th century, we would not expect these creatures to have been called by that name. Instead, we would expect to find that they were called by other names. That's why we find

Figure #133. YE OL' DRAGON

the names dragon and monster in the ancient manuscripts.

Ye Ol' Dragon.

At some point in Earth's history, dragons came to be known as symbols of evil and destruction. It is of special interest that translators of the King James Version of the Bible translated the Hebrew word "tanniym" as "dragon(s)" more than 20 times in the Old Testament such as:

- Ezekiel 29:3 — Metaphorically speaking of Pharaoh
- Psalm 91:13 — Referring to animals
- Jeremiah 9:11 — Jerusalem becoming a den of dragons

Keep in mind that the KJV was published in 1611, a time when people were well aware of the many historical accounts of the existence of such creatures. The amazing significance of these references is that they were only made about 400 years ago, and they were made by translators attempting to give meaningful language to the common people of their day.

There are many stories of people killing dragons during the first 1,000 years after the Flood. Such legends can be found around the world in Asia, Africa, Europe and the Middle East. **(See fig. #134.)** In the book by Paul S. Taylor titled *The Great*

Figure #134. DINO DOCUMENTATION

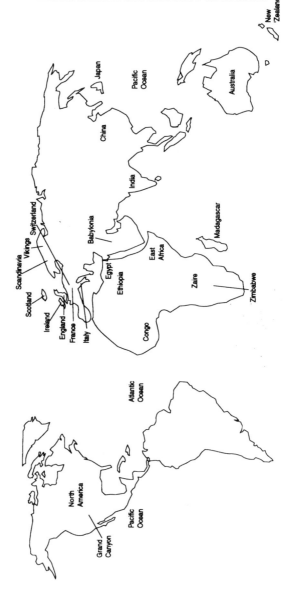

Dinosaur Mystery and the Bible[16] and the motion picture "The Great Dinosaur Mystery,"[17] numerous eye witness reports of dinosaurs throughout history have been researched and recorded. Some of the following accounts occurred in different time periods and diverse places.

Nimrod, the Mighty Hunter.

The first great event recorded in the Bible after the Flood was the construction of the Tower of Babel. About 300 years had elapsed since the Flood, and Nimrod had risen to power. His kingdom lasted for several hundred years — until about 2200 B.C., according to historians.

The tower was more than just a great physical structure. It was a symbol of power and of man's ability to save himself from any future worldwide disaster. God was thoroughly displeased with this project because it was done in rebellion. In fact, Nimrod's name means "let us rebel."[18]

Nimrod was a man who was apparently gifted in some extraordinary ways. He was a person of high popularity in his day. The Bible maintains that he was a mighty hunter. Could it be that he had hunted down some of the great monsters of the dinosaur kingdom that by then had sufficient time to begin reproducing and growing to their gigantic size?

Babylonia (2000 B.C.).

The Babylonians have one of the oldest accounts of a monster named Khumbaba. It was a huge reptilian creature that was killed in a forest in ancient Sumer, the southern division of old Babylonia.[19] The account is recorded in the Epic of Gilgamesh. Also, fifth-century B.C. Babylonian records tell of live dragons in captivity. The people worshiped them. In 600 B.C., Nebuchadnezzar had as a symbol the god Marduk on top of a fire-breathing dragon. Marduk was the creator in the Babylonian story of creation.

It is interesting that in the Catholic Bible, in one of the two chapters in Daniel not in the Protestant Bible, there is a story in which Daniel slays a dragon that was in the palace at Babylon. Babylon was eventually destroyed in 500 B.C. Centuries later, the walls were discovered in the sand. They had carvings of lions and the Babylonian dragon, which had a long neck and a long tail.

Africa (Fourth Century B.C.).

Herodotus, a Greek historian and explorer, tells about flying reptiles in Egypt. From his description, it sounds like they were Rhamphorhynchus. These bat-like creatures had snake-like bodies and wings. Herodotus saw many of the bones of these flying reptiles which had been killed. **(See fig. #135.)** Aristotle, the Greek philosopher, also made reference to such creatures existing in Ethiopia.

Figure #135. PTERANODON PTOOTLING OVER THE PYRAMIDS

India (Third Century B.C.).

Alexander the Great records an event that took place when he and his army were in India. A 100-foot dragon came out of a cave and made a terrible hissing noise.

China.

The Chinese have been influenced significantly by their legends of dragons. There are literally thousands of accounts throughout China's history about dragons. Paintings, statues and illustrations abound in Chinese art, so much so, that the dragon has become China's national symbol. Records going back to long before the time of Christ reveal the Chinese had numerous encounters with dragons. Legend has it that on stately occasions, dragons were used to tow the royal chariots of the noble. **(See fig. #136.)** And the Chinese designed their ships after dragons of the sea.

Scandinavia.

The Vikings had dragon heads on their ships. Among the many legends of the Scandinavians, there is an account of a creature which had a body of an ox, only it was covered with scales, and its front legs were different from the back ones. The rear legs were like a frog's, while the front legs

Figure #136. DRAGON POWER

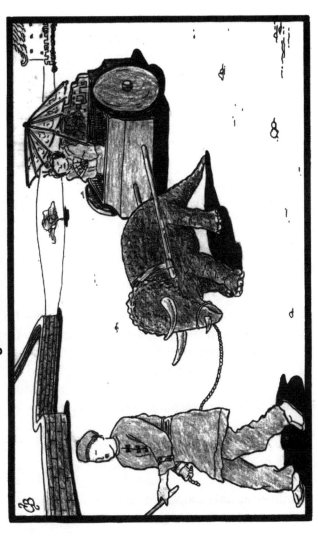

were short. Its mouth was the frightening aspect of its appearance; it had immense jaws. There are several dinosaurs which have similar characteristics — the well-known and ferocious-looking Tyrannosaurs rex **(see fig. #59)**, and the not-so- well-known Iguanodon **(see fig. #5)**, and the Edmontosaurus.

Early Britain.

The King of Wales in 336 B.C., King Morvidus, was killed and eaten by a reptilian monster.[20]

East Anglia, England (Seventh Century A.D.)

An Anglo Saxon poem from around A.D. 495-583 tells of the Scandinavian Beowulf killing a monstrous creature named Grendel. The description of the reptilian monster is amazingly close to a dinosaur. **(See fig. #137.)** It stood on two legs and had small forearms, which Beowulf was able to dismember. The creature slew its prey with its jaws and mouth. Its skin was so tough that a sword had a difficult time penetrating it.[21]

During his life, Beowulf fought and killed numerous other reptilian monsters, until he met his death in a battle against a flying reptile at the

Figure #137. DUELING DRAGONS

ripe old age of 88. The description of the flying creature fits closely to that of the Pteranodon — the giant flying reptilian lizard. **(See fig. #66.)**[22]

There are numerous other legendary accounts of the ancient Britains slaying dragons, including King Arthur, Sir Lancelot, and St. George, who became a saint of England. No doubt many of these accounts were about real monsters that lived and were slain. However, over the years, many of the stories, and even illustrations depicting the encounters, have been embellished. These fanciful additions make them seem unreal.

On the other hand, what further substantiates the validity of many of these ancient reports is the lack of embellishment. Many of the accounts are told in a matter-of-fact historical approach rather than the kind of tale that can be read today in a children's book of fairy tales, which has the element of fantasy.

Still, because there are so many stories of dinosaurs from around the world, we can assume that in the past, there must have been real creatures with such size and strength that they brought fear to the hearts of people who encountered them. Many of these creatures fit the descriptions of known dinosaur fossils.

Ireland (10th Century).

There is an account by an ancient Irish author of a creature which sounds like the dinosaur Stegosaurus. **(See fig. #138.)** Like Stegosaurus, the creature had spikes on its tail which pointed backward, and it had a head that resembled a horse. It also had massive legs with iron-like claws.[23]

Figure #138. STEGOSAURUS

Madagascar (13th Century).

The famous explorer, Marco Polo, gives an account of a large bird living on the island of Madagascar (in the Indian Ocean off Southeast

Africa). This account was considered a legend until 1967, when the remains of these birds' bones and eggs were discovered. The remains reveal the birds were over 10 feet tall. **(See fig. #139.)**[24]

The significance of this and other discoveries is substantial. The legends about creatures of the past, which have been rejected by the evolutionary community because they think such creatures never existed or have been extinct for millions of years, are in fact strong evidence that the evolutionary dogma is really illusionary.

Italy (16th Century).

Early Roman mosaics show dragons fighting, and as late as A.D. 1500, encounters with dinosaurs were still being documented. A prominent book of science from that period, *Historia Animaliom*, stated that dinosaurs were still living, but very rare. Ulysses Aldervandes, a famous scientist, recorded the slaying of a rare dragon on May 15, 1572 by a peasant named Baptista. Ulysses sent for the creature's body and after receiving it, took measurements, made a drawing and mounted the creature's head for a museum. It had a very long neck and tail, with a large body. The description is very similar to the Tanastrophias **(see fig. #140)**, which is a creature relatively small in stature.[25]

Figure #139. BIG BIRD OF MADAGASCAR STREET

Figure #140. TANASTROPHIAS

Switzerland.

The famous Swiss naturalist and town doctor, Conrad Gessner, from the 1500s, describes and illustrates various dragons in his book of snakes, *Schlangenbuch*. He also describes a battle between a Swiss man and a dragon which took place near the Swiss village of Wyler. According to the story, in the early days of Swiss settlement, a cruel dragon lived above the village of Wyler, and drove out men and cattle. A countryman called Winkelried, who had been banished for murder, offered to kill the dragon in exchange for freedom and being allowed to return. He did manage to kill the dragon, but apparently lost his life in the process.[26] The story was illustrated in *Mundus Subterraneus* by the Jesuit scholar, Athanasius Kircher, in 1678.

France (19th Century).

From France, there is an account which involves the city of Nerluc, which was renamed in tribute of the slaying of a dragon-like beast. The monster was somewhat larger than an ox and had spiked horns above its skull. Triceratops fits the description. **(See fig. #141.)**[27]

According to a report in *The Illustrated London News* of February 9, 1856, some workmen digging a railway tunnel in France between

Figure #141. TRICERATOPS

Nancy and St. Dizier, disturbed a strange creature when they used gunpowder to blow up an enormous block of stone for the tunnel at Culmont in Haute Marne. They described the creature as having a very long neck and sharp teeth. It was livid black, and it looked like a bat. Its membranous skin was thick and oily. On reaching the light, the creature gave some signs of life by shaking its wings, but it died soon after, uttering a hoarse cry. Its wingspan was measured at 3.22 meters, or about 10 feet, 7 inches.

A naturalist well versed in paleontology "immediately recognized it as belonging to the genus Perodactylus Anas." The living creature was said to have matched the many fossil remains of Pterodactyls which had been found, so it was dubbed a "living fossil."

Germany (20th Century).

There is still a ceremony of "dragon-slaying" in a festival held yearly in the small town of Furth im Wald in Eastern Bavaria, Germany. This involves a large, fire-spewing dragon being killed by a knight. Every August, the dragon is ritually "killed" by a prince on horseback. Whether the ceremony actually depicts a historical event, we cannot be sure; however, the celebration does depict what Christ has done over the king of dragons.

In another small German village in the Bavarian Alps, Oberammergau, the citizens celebrate the Passion Play of Christ's life, death and resurrection every 10 years. They do so in memory of answered prayer in 1634 when the black plague stopped short of their town after taking the lives of three-fourths of the people of Europe.

Chapter Twenty-Eight

Flying Dragons of Recent Times

Switzerland (17th Century).

Did the Pterodactyls die out some 65 million years ago as evolutionists believe? Or did they survive the Flood in Noah's Ark and die out in more recent days? A 17th-century Anglo-Saxon chronicle reported a reptilian-like bird flying near Mt. Pilatus near Lucerne, Switzerland in 1619. The description closely resembles the ancient lizard-bird, the Perodactylus. The creature reportedly flew out of a cave on Mount Pilatus and flapped across the valley with slowly beating wings. Athanasius Kircher depicted the creature that was printed on the map of Switzerland in *Mattaeus Seutter's Atlas of the World* as late as 1730. **(See fig. #142.)**

British Explorers.

Even as recently as early 1900, a report came

Figure #142. PTERODACTYL

from four English explorers led by the famous London zoologist, Professor George Edward Challenger. The group came upon what they reported as a living Pterosaurus in South America. The account was related by Ed Malone one of the team members and reporter for the *Daily Gazette*.

Malone describes their encounter with the prehistoric creature in the following manner.

> We saw, at the distance of a mile or so, something appeared to be a huge grey bird flap slowly up from the ground and skim smoothly off, flying very low and straight, until it was lost among tree-ferns.

On the same evening, they were to make an even closer acquaintance with Pterosaur. ... The men were sitting around the camp fire roasting an aguti, a small pig-like animal, that Lord Roxton had killed for their supper. But let Ed Malone tell us himself:

> The night was moonless, but there were some stars, and one could see for a little distance across the plain. Well, suddenly out of the darkness, out of the night, there swooped something with a swish like an aeroplane. The

whole group of us were covered for an instant by a canopy of leathery wings, and I had a momentary vision of a long, snake-like neck, a fierce, red greedy eye, and a great snapping beak, filled, to my amazement, with little gleaming teeth. The next instant it was gone — and so was our dinner. A huge black shadow, twenty feet across, skimmed up into the air; for an instant the monster's wings blotted out the stars, and then it vanished over the brow of the cliffs above us.[28]

The story becomes even more interesting when it relates how one of the reptilian birds was captured and taken to England, where it was witnessed by a number of invited guests who had assembled at a meeting of the Royal Zoological Society. Unfortunately, the bird escaped through an open window. Later, a sighting was discovered in the log of the S. S. Friesland Steamer of the Dutch-America Line. The ship's log describes the creature as looking like something between a flying goat and a monstrous bat.

Whether or not the story is true, we cannot be sure. However, in the 60 years since the story was published, many fossilized remains of the Ptero-

saurs have been found on the high plateau in
North-Eastern Brazil, the same plateau where the
report stated that the creature had been seen. The
fossils revealed a creature just like the one
described with "a long, snake-like neck ... a great
snapping beak, filled ... with little gleaming
teeth."

Flying Dragons.

Flying reptilian fossils were first discovered
in the 18th century, and many have been found
since. Their dimensions range from the size of a
modern-day bat to the size of small plane. Pteranodon means "winged, toothless." Evolutionists have no logical explanation to the origin of
these creatures, but the Bible does.

> And God said, "Let the water teem
> with living creatures, and let birds fly
> above the earth across the expanse of
> the sky." So God created the great
> creatures of the sea and every living
> and moving thing with which the
> water teems, according to their kinds,
> and every winged bird according to its
> kind. And God saw that it was good.
> God blessed them and said, "Be fruit-
> ful and increase in number and fill the

water in the seas, and let the birds increase on the earth." And there was evening, and there was morning — the fifth day (Gen. 1:20-23).

If many of these creatures were in fact mammals, like bats, then verses 24 and 25 declare their creation.

Accounts of sightings of flying dragons have been reported throughout history, yet if it weren't for the fossils of such creatures being found, modern man might believe that such stories were only myths. For example, Greek historian Herodotus of the fifth century, wrote that he had witnessed "winged serpents" in Arabia. The description fits that of the Pterodactyls. Similar reports come from Africa, Asia, Europe and even America. Some people living in Africa claim these flying creatures still exist. They have come to be called "Kongamato."

Ancestors of the Ford Thunderbird.

North American Indians from Mexico to Alaska have legends of huge flying creatures, one of which has become known as the Thunderbird, a name which was given to describe the noise it made while flapping its wings during flight.

The Sioux Indians have a legend of a huge bird sighted by a hunting party; the bird was struck by lightning. It fits the description of the Pterodactyl. **(See fig. #142.)** It had large talons on its feet as well as one on its wings. Its beak was elongated and pointed, and it had a bony crest on its head. The hunters had never come upon any such creature previously. It came to be known as the "thunderbird," which the Ford Motor Company acquired for the name of one of its sports cars.

Who Killed Quetzalcoatlus? (See fig. #143.)

An interesting article was carried in the *Tombstone Epitaph* on April 26, 1890. The report told of two cowboys who were riding horseback outside of Tombstone, Arizona, when they spotted a giant flying creature which they described as having a long, slender body with claws on its wings and feet. Its head was several feet long, and looked much like that of an alligator. It had teeth in its beak, and its eyes protruded. After it landed, the men killed it and cut off the tip of its wing for a souvenir. The wing was smooth and tough like a bat's.[29]

This amazing story may in fact be more than just a wild tale as it fits the description of a member of the Pteranodon family of flying rep-

Figure #143. QUETZALCOATLUS

tiles, and resembles the description of the Quetzalcoatlus fossil that was discovered in the panhandle of Texas in 1972. Could it be that these two fellows killed one of the last remaining lizard birds in existence just over 100 years ago?

Pterodactyl Hits the Skies and Ground.

As amazing and mysterious as these flying creatures may have been, it is hard to envision just how magnificent they actually were. So man has attempted to manufacture one. A radio-controlled model of the Pterodactyl, which has a 15-foot wingspan, took to the skies in 1988. It took its inventor, Stephen Winkworth, eight years and hundreds of thousands of dollars to get it perfected, then on its first public demonstration it flew for only a few minutes before crashing to the ground. This shows how marvelously the Creator designed the real Pterodactyls.

Still Alive?

Although most of the huge reptilian birds were destroyed during the Flood, there is a scientist who may have found evidence that a few of these creatures could still be alive. He has discovered that natives living in Zimbabwe have seen a strange flying animal they call the "Kongamato," living mainly in the Jiunda Swamp —

a huge, dense area. They did not perceive it as a bird, but more of a reddish lizard with bat-like wings approximately seven feet long from wing-tip to wingtip. When the natives were shown pictures of various types of living and extinct creatures, every one of them chose the Pterodactyl as looking like the creature they saw. We can never say a creature is extinct, because there just might come a day when one has been spotted, as we shall see.

Chapter Twenty-Nine

Living Dinosaurs

Are There Any Dinosaurs Alive Today?

Dinosaurs are thought to have become extinct. But from time to time evidence surfaces that a few of them may still be alive.

Australia.

The aborigines of Australia report having sighted a creature which looks like Struthiomimus **(see fig. #144)**, a creature somewhat like an ostrich, but without wings or feathers.

Africa.

From Africa there have been numerous accounts over the years of large creatures that are similar to the Sauropod herb-eating dinosaurs such as the Brachiosaurus, Apatosaurus and the Diplodocus. **(See fig. #145.)** Rumors persist that such a creature may still be alive in the dense, swampy parts of Zaire.

Figure #144. STRUTHIOMIMUS

Figure #145. ALIVE IN AFRICA?

In Zaire, located in Central Africa, in a remote unexplored area of thick swamp jungle populated with poisonous varmints and fierce pygmies, there has been sighted an animal which the pygmies described as being a reddish-brown reptile about the size of a hippopotamus, with a long neck and a snakelike head. There are also plants living in the area that according to the evolutionary theory have been extinct for about 65 million years.

In 1993, an article was carried in the *Australian Newcastle Herald* (12/29/93) which claimed that such a creature had been sighted continually by the natives, and that even some Westerners have attested to seeing the lizard-like reptile. The natives' name for the creature, which closely resembles the Apatosaurus, is mokele-mbembe.

Over the last two centuries, occasional visitors to this unexplored part of Zaire have returned with incredible stories. They all confirm the natives are absolutely honest in their reports of the "mokele-mbembe" (mo-kel-ly-mm-bembe). They say these animals are huge, with small heads, long necks, and lengthy massive tails; they wade in slow meandering rivers, and have been described as "half elephant and half dragon."

Further interviews with the natives revealed

astonishing accounts. About 30 years ago some of them managed to spear to death one of the creatures. All those who ate the flesh are said to have died soon afterward. When shown pictures of various large animals, living and extinct, the pygmies verified the Brachiosaurus as most like what they call mokele-mbembe.

One creature was captured on film swimming upstream in a wide river and was shown a few years ago in the United States on the national TV program, *That's Incredible*. A few years ago in Zaire, there was great excitement over another report of a large reptile similar to the Brachiosaurus. In an exclusive report in the April 1982 *Bible-Science Newsletter*, Dr. John Look, a missionary-dentist in the remote region near Lake Tele, offered evidence that the creature is real and that it resembles a dinosaur. The local natives, who worship the creatures (there seem to be several), identified them with the Brachiosaurus illustration they were shown in a book. Dr. Look has since come to the conclusion there is a small family of dinosaurs living in the Lake Tele region, one of the most remote tropical regions of Earth.

A few expeditions have been organized in recent years to try to verify the reports, but they have been unsuccessful. There are swamps in

Africa that cover more than 55,000 square miles, which is an area bigger than the state of Arkansas.

Grand Canyon Graffiti. (See fig. #146.)

Here's one final report of recent dinosaur sightings: carvings on the side of a cliff some 30-40 feet above ground level on the sandstone walls in the Grand Canyon. The carvings have eroded very little and are about 19 inches in size; they seem to be crude carvings of what look like the Tyrannosaurs or Allosaurus and the Brachiosaurus.

Ancient man left messages in the stone in the form of rock art. These pictures challenge the evolutionary theory of time. There are also carvings of people and of animals such as goats, horses, elephants, woolly rhinoceros' and the ibex. The Havasupai Indians claim the carvings have been there since before they first inhabited the canyon centuries ago.

Findings of "Extinct" Species Baffle Scientists.

On the walls of the Grand Canyon, not only are there carved images of dinosaurs, but also of extinct mammals. Evolutionists once believed that the mammoth (see fig. #147) became extinct about 40,000 years ago. However, pictographs

Figure #146. DINOSAUR GRAFFITI

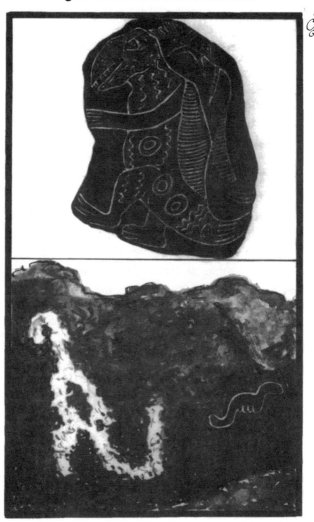

Figure #147. MAMMOTH

left by the Anaxazi Indians, who lived from about 150 B.C. to A.D. 1500 in the southwestern United States, reveal that they were hunting these creatures. That means they existed much more recently than the evolutionists thought.

Near Moab, Utah, a pictograph of a mammoth reveals all of its features, distinguishing it clearly. The pictograph shows the four skeletal toes which are characteristic of mammoths, whereas elephants living today have five. According to evolutionism, no Indian at that time should have ever seen a mammoth. Even if the Indians knew about the mammoth because they happened to come upon a skeleton of the mammoth, they would never have known about the trunk. There are numerous other examples of pictographs throughout Utah and Colorado. Of course, a student of the Bible is not surprised because these creatures no doubt lived after the Flood, and some of them may have only recently died out. In fact, reports like those of mokele-mbembe indicate there may be a few still living.

These reports pose serious problems for the evolutionary paleontologist, for they have taught that dinosaurs became extinct millions of years ago — long before man evolved. It appears dinosaurs lived far more recently than evolutionists supposed; they probably began to gradually fade from the scene after the Flood due to environmental conditions.

In addition to the discoveries of dinosaurs, there are continuous findings of other so-called extinct species, both plant and animal.

Chapter Thirty

Living Monsters From the Sea

Scotland.

Probably the most well-known "monster" is the creature that has been seen in the Loch Ness, Scotland. Loch Ness is a large inland lake, extremely deep and murky, which cuts across Scotland and fills a massive geological fault. The description of the creature (or creatures) resembles the water dinosaurs, Plesiosaurs **(see fig. #148)**, whose long necks, more than twice the

Figure #148. PLESIOSAURUS

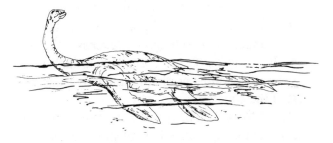

length of their bodies, have been found fossilized in rocks. Some as long as 55 feet have been discovered.

One description was a snake strung through the body of a turtle. This creature has been sighted occasionally for centuries in the Loch. It even has been captured on film numerous times; however, the quality of the photos leaves much to be desired. The Plesiosaur it resembles has been extinct for at least 70 million years according to evolutionism .

National Geographic Institution has expended much effort trying to establish the truth of these reports, using all of the latest scientific technology. However, because of the great depth and length of the Loch, it's like trying to find a needle in a haystack — blindfolded!

The Loch Ness (**see fig. #149**) stretches 24 miles in length and in some places is more than 900 feet deep. It has over 100 rivers and streams feeding into it. The lake is filled with tiny particles, so that all but the top few feet of water is virtually impenetrable by light. Along its shores, the mountains rise to heights in excess of 2,000 feet. It lies in the Great Glen, a wide fault line dividing Scotland's northern highlands from the rest of the country.

Loch Ness is believed to have been open to the sea in the past; a geological shift created the

Figure #149. LOCH NESS

narrow isthmus that keeps it landlocked today. It is to this geological shift Nessie supporters like to point, conjecturing that several seagoing beasts were caught in the Loch, adapted and continued to breed. With the Loch Ness being large and remote, and being that it offered a plentiful supply of salmon, brown and sea trout, Arctic char and eels, it provides an ideal habitat for a herd of large predatory animals.

The first documented sighting recorded of a "certain water monster" in Loch Ness goes back to A.D. 565, to an account by an early Christian missionary, Saint Columba. More sightings occurred through the centuries, but Nessie remained largely a regional legend until 1933, when a road was completed along the length of Loch Ness' northwest shore. Once people were able to visit the area easily, tourist sightings added to the legend. Over 400 recorded sightings have occurred since 1900, and that makes more than 3,000 sightings over the last 1,400 years. All of these testimonies suggest that there is something very interesting yet to be identified in the Loch.

Japan.

The enormous reptilian creatures of the oceans could have survived the Flood without being taken on the Ark, just like the great sea creatures that are common in today's seas did. Interestingly, there have been many reports from sailors on seagoing vessels about one particular creature which fits the description of the Plesiosaurus.

In fact, in 1977, a rare situation occurred with a Japanese fishing vessel, the Zuiyo Maru, which netted the body of a massive strange creature near New Zealand. Some scientists believe it to have been the carcass of a Plesiosaurs. **(See fig. #150.)** A zoologist on board took careful measurements, specimens and pictures before returning the decomposing carcass to the sea so as not to contaminate their large cargo of fish. The carcass measured 32 feet long and weighed about 4,000 pounds.

The photos, samples and report of the zoologist were inspected and analyzed by a group of Japanese marine scientists. The Director of Animal Research at the National Science Museum of Japan stated, "It seems that these animals are not extinct after all. It's impossible for only one to have survived. There must be a group."

The discovery made such an impression on the Japanese government that it was commemorated on a postage stamp as the scientific discovery of the year. **(See fig. #151.)** It also led to the Plesiosaur being used as the Japanese official

Figure #150. 65-MILLION-YEAR-OLD CARCASS

emblem of the 1977 National Exhibition, which celebrated 100 years of scientific discovery. The Japanese scientists had no cause to doubt the authenticity of the find. The Western world, however, took a more skeptical view.

Figure #151. STAMPS OF APPROVAL

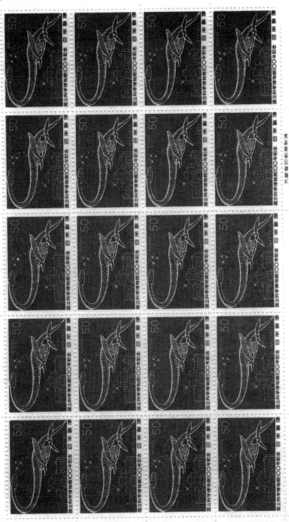

国立科学博物館一〇〇年記念

This discovery was largely ignored by the Western scientific world because of evolutionary bias. It is amazing how evolutionists, who were never within a thousand miles of the carcass, could totally ignore the eye-witness reports and the studies of Japanese scientists who analyzed the samples of this fantastic discovery.

Why did scientists of the Western world basically ignore the discovery? Could it be because so many are committed philosophically to the evolutionary assumption that these types of creatures became extinct 60-70 million years ago? With that mindset, they cannot believe that it is possible they could be found today. Therefore, they decided it must have been a sea mammal or a type of shark — even though this conclusion was contrary to scientific data.

Preconceived ideas always win out. Those who are prepared to believe in the possibility of living Plesiosauri existing today were convinced, or nearly so, while those who refused to believe found nothing in this solid evidence to change their minds.

Oceans of the World.

Reports from all around the world continue to tell of creatures which were sighted, but are not identified as any kind of marine life living today.

It is widely held by scientists that there are still creatures yet to be discovered and known to mankind.

One sighting came from the U.S.S. Stein, a Navy ship, which encountered a creature that apparently ruined the ship's sonar equipment after it became fastened to the ship's bottom. After the ship's return to the Naval Dockyard in Long Beach, California, it was discovered that the solid dome which housed the sonar equipment had been ripped and lacerated, with huge gouges left in the covering. After months of investigation, scientists at the Naval Station concluded the creature that had come in contact with the ship was extremely large, but they could not identify it.[30]

World War I Creature of the Sea.

Another encounter with a large unidentified sea creature occurred during World War I. It was described by George von Forstner, who was the captain of a German U-boat. Captain von Forstner reported the following:

> On 30 July 1915, our U28 torpedoed the British steamer Iberian carrying a rich cargo in the North Atlantic. The steamer sank quickly, the bow sticking

almost vertically into the air. When it had been gone for about twenty-five seconds, there was a violent explosion. A little later, pieces of wreckage, and among them a gigantic sea animal, writhing and struggling wildly, was shot out of the water to a height of 60 to 100 feet. At that moment I had with me in the conning tower my officer of the watch, the chief engineer, the navigator, and the helmsman. ... We did not have the time to take a photograph, for the animal sank out of sight after ten or fifteen seconds. It was about 60 feet long, was like a crocodile in shape, and had four limbs with powerful webbed feet, and a long tail tapering to a point.[31]

One of the largest crocodiles ever harpooned was taken off the Northern coast of Australia. It wasn't even half of the size of the monster described by the German officer. It measured only about 20 feet.

The Coelacanth: A "Living Fossil."
(See fig. #152.)

The coelacanth, a six-foot fish, was discovered a few decades ago being eaten by the natives

Figure #152. COELACANTH: A "LIVING FOSSIL"

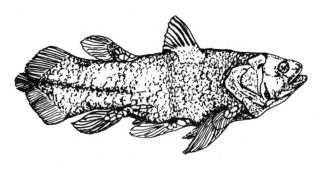

of East Africa; they had apparently been doing so for generations. The reason the discovery of the coelacanth was such news is that the fish was supposed to have been extinct for 60 or 70 million years — according to the evolutionists' inflated dating of the Earth. Using the evolutionists' scale, the coelacanth supposedly became extinct during the same general period that dinosaurs did.

Creationists know that all creatures alive today are descended from creatures which survived the Flood. That is why they are not surprised to find the coelacanth is still around. According to the evolutionists, it was a "primitive" fish because fossilized examples showed it had lobes shaped sort of like paddles instead of fins, which most fish have. These lobe-like paddles led evolutionists to imagine the coelacanth was a creature on the way to evolving into an amphibian. They assumed the lobes were fins on the way to becoming legs.

In 1987, *National Geographic* sent several scientists on an expedition to find a live coelacanth. After much work, they discovered where these fish lived. They learned that these fish catch food by electrical currents, often standing on their heads for as long as two minutes. Also, these fish do not walk on their fins as claimed by evolutionists. The coelacanth is a modern-day fish; it needs its shape and form to survive in an environment with much pressure.

More than 100 of coelacanth have been caught. When the first living specimen was found and later examined in 1938, Professor J.L.B. Smith at South Africa's Rhodes University confirmed the coelacanth were still alive. He said, "My surprise would have been little greater if I had seen a dinosaur walking down the street."

As these so-called "extinct" creatures surface from obscurity, they baffle evolutionists. Although most dinosaurs have become extinct, there may be some still existing in the depths of the oceans or in the uninhabited remote jungles. In time, some of them may be captured — at least on film. One thing is for sure: The evidence is overwhelming that man and dinosaur lived together in bygone times, and even in the recent past.

With more and more improvements in scientific investigation, there is mounting evidence that legends of sea monsters may have been real. The Bible describes such monsters as real creatures numerous times.

Chapter Thirty-One

More Amazing Discoveries

Blood, Bones and Bark

Fresh Dinosaur Soup. (See fig. #153.)

Have you ever had chicken or turkey soup that was made from the bones left after a scrumptious Thanksgiving dinner? My family does every year. My mom never throws out the bones of the turkey because she can always provide an additional meal with the savory broth which comes from boiling the bones for several hours. The broth, with some noodles and seasoning added, always goes well with left over turkey sandwiches after Thanksgiving.

Would you believe that now it is possible to do the same with dinosaur bones? Not with fossilized bones, but frozen ones. That's right, dinosaur bones that haven't been fossilized have recently been discovered in Alaska.[32]

I'm not sure I would want to be the guinea pig

Figure #153. CAMPFIRE VITTLES:
DINOSAUR SOUP

to taste the first bowl of "yucky-saurus" soup. But I have a gnawing question in the back of my mind. How is it possible for bones to be fresh if all the dinosaurs have been dead for 65 million years, as the evolutionists claim? Can bones remain in a fresh, organic condition for 65 million years without becoming fossilized — or fertilizer? The answer is no — unless the bones are not 65 million years old, of course.

Fresh dinosaur bones have been found, not only in Alaska, but also in Canada. These bones have been identified as those of the duckbilled dinosaur. **(See fig. #154.)** How about some Duckbill dinosaur stew.[33]

Some think that the bones have been preserved by the snow and ice over the years. The only problem with that idea is that, according to evolutionism, the dinosaurs didn't live at a time when there was snow and ice. They supposedly lived in a warm and tropical environment. Even after the dinosaurs died out, it is an evolutionary assumption that the Earth was still quite warm as a result of high levels of CO_2 in the atmosphere. Then how do they explain the fresh bones?

How About Fresh Tree Bark?

Well, the same question can be asked about the fresh (unfossilized) timber that is supposed

Figure #154. DUCKBILL DINOSAUR

to be 45 million years dead, but is well preserved.[34] This timber was discovered only about 800 miles from the North Pole. The area was once particularly lush — with trees that were 150 feet in length and six feet in diameter. The logs aren't petrified, and could be cut and used as logs for cooking the fresh dinosaur bones to make our Duckbill dinosaur stew.

Of course, the answer to this dilemma is that the evolutionary timetable is pure speculation. It was concocted because it was needed to support a philosophy and religion that rejects the God of creation. The evidence from both the fresh bones and timber reveal that the creation of the Earth was a recent event.

Dinosaur Food Still Fresh. (See fig. #155.)

In addition to the living coelacanth, there are other surprises for the evolutionary camp. Recently discovered are the William pine trees found in the Blue Mountains of Australia. (Some are 115 feet in height.) The trees had been previously dubbed living fossils because evolutionists believe they died off some 150 million years ago. Fossils of these trees are not found in any layers of rock that are considered younger. They are completely missing from the evolutionary fossil record for the last 150 million years. Where

Figure #155. SURPLUS DINOSAUR DELIGHTS

did they go? Nowhere. They are and always have been with us. It's just that it is only recently that they were found. Here is another example of the erroneous evolutionary chart that supposedly tells when creatures and plants lived, died and became extinct. Once again their chart is in error — by 150 million years.

Furthermore, the living specimens are just like those found fossilized, further revealing the mistaken nature of evolutionism which states that there should be significant change in something over such a vast stretch of time. In other words, why didn't this tree evolve? The bottom line is that this is just one more discovery which casts doubt on the entire evolutionary time line and the age of the dinosaurs. This blow, like all the others, points to the fact that the evolutionary geological chart of ages is nothing more than 20th century mythology or at best science fiction.

The Blood of Dinosaurs: Found!

Recently, traces of the blood protein hemoglobin were found in some fossil bones of a Tyrannosaurs rex. These red blood cells are the carriers of oxygen. This is incredible if dinosaurs have been extinct for 65 million years as evolutionists claim. Yet this is no surprise for one who believes the Bible, which teaches that dinosaurs are only a few thousand years old.

The exciting news comes from the Montana State University, where scientists are studying the partially fossilized remains of a T-rex discovered in 1990. The report points out the bones are not completely fossilized, which is also incredible. If all this turns out to be 100 percent accurate, then evolutionism will suffer another major blow to its imaginary foundation which is based on billions of years that never existed. Here is another powerful testimony against the evolutionary belief that dinosaurs lived millions of years ago. It is also a powerful testimony in favor of the Bible's account of a recent creation of the dinosaur family.

Oh, no! Hollywood may have another reason to produce a monster movie, now that the fresh blood can supply the DNA to reproduce a T-rex. Will it ever end?

Chapter Thirty-Two

Why Dinosaurs Are Extinct: The Evolutionary Speculation

Over the years, evolutionists have contrived a variety of bizarre explanations as to what led to the mass extinction of the dinosaurs, such as:

- Rodents ate their eggs
- Low IQ
- Boredom
- Starvation
- Overeating
- Became blind from cataracts
- Shrinking brain resulting in greater stupidity
- Mass suicide
- Sunspots
- Being overweight led to slipped disks
- Worldwide heat wave — 2 degree increase — caused males to become sterile

- Poisonous plants
- Constipation
- Cosmic catastrophe

Grasping for Straws.

It is obvious that evolutionism doesn't have a clue what killed the dinosaurs. A good example of how evolutionists are simply grasping for straws is this quote from a recent book on dinosaurs.

> Now comes the important question. What caused all these extinctions at one particular point in time, approximately 65 million years ago? Dozens of reasons have been suggested, some serious and sensible, others quite crazy, and yet others merely as a joke. Every year people come up with new theories on this thorny problem. The trouble is that if we are to find just one reason to account for them all, it would have to explain the death, all at the same time, of animals living on land and of animals living in the sea; but, in both cases, of only some of those animals, for many of the land dwellers and many of the sea-dwellers went on living quite happily into the following period. Alas, no such one explanation exists.[35]

Cosmic Catastrophe.

Figure #156. *TIME* MAGAZINE'S FEATURE ARTICLE

Of all the 50 plus theories concocted by the evolutionists as to the cause for the extinction of the dinosaurs, the cosmic catastrophe has become the most popular of late.

Several years ago, an issue of *Time* (5/6/85)

magazine featured a cover story of a new theory attempting to give yet another explanation for the mysterious extinction of the dinosaurs. The *Time* cover asks: "Did comets kill the dinosaurs?" Supporters of this theory believe they have evidence that validates a cosmic catastrophe on Earth in the past when a six-mile-wide meteorite plunged into the surface of the Earth. **(See fig. #157.)**

Figure #157. METEORITE IMPACT

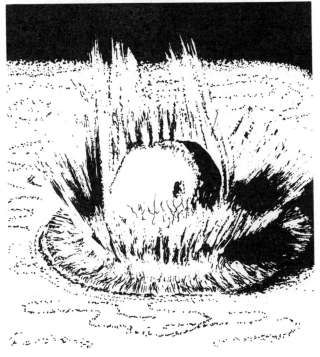

It is suggested that tremendous meteoric impact raised so much dust that the sky darkened, the Earth's temperatures dropped, and the reptiles died of frostbite. *Time* reported, "Whether these catastrophic impacts are random or cyclic remains to be seen. But if they occur at all, they could shake the foundations of evolutionary biology." This hypothesis presents a major break with the long-held evolutionary theory. As *Time* put it, "All these fanciful concepts fail to account for the hundreds of other species that perished at the end of the cretaceous." At the University of California, a Berkeley physicist, Luis Alverez, says, "The problem is not what killed the dinosaurs but what killed almost all the life at the time?" Genesis chapter six reveals the answer: the Flood.

Missing Hole the Size of New York City.

If such a catastrophic meteorite impact did occur on planet Earth, how is it that the site has yet to be positively verified? Evolutionary scientists are having a problem with locating the crater hole. The place which many evolutionists have agreed upon is located in Mexico on the Yucatan Peninsula, but leaves many questions unanswered. **(See fig. #158.)**

An additional problem with the mysterious cos-

Figure #158. SUPPOSED IMPACT SITE

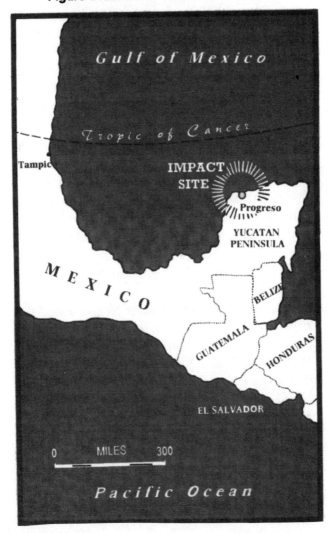

mic crash is the survival of the more fragile creatures. How did birds, many small mammals, and other reptiles — like turtles, snakes and alligators — make it? If the meteorite episode really happened, how did so many other creatures survive the worldwide effects of the blast? Would it be too ridiculous to suggest that maybe they had been forewarned and were in a fallout shelter?

The reason evolutionists give for their belief in this catastrophe from space is that traces of a metal called iridium have been found in some layers of clay around the Earth. Meteorites contain this metal, and evolutionists believe a meteor to be the source of this iridium. However, the Earth's core has this metal in it as well, and it is sometimes brought up by erupting volcanoes.

Creation scientists consider Noah's Flood to be what caused the Earth to experience by far the most far-reaching, worldwide catastrophe ever. Earthquakes and volcanic eruptions were taking place by the thousands during and long after the Flood year. This could easily have produced a layer of dust containing iridium in the atmosphere. The dust would have eventually fallen to the Earth and been buried throughout the massive layers of clay, mud and sand forming the stratum of the Earth. Such layers of sediment, containing fossils of creatures that were entombed by the millions, surely provides reasonable evidence for some worldwide cataclysmic event which caused the death and extinction of the dinosaur kingdom. Only a remnant would have been saved — those which were on the Ark.

Time concludes its article with a cynical and skillfully misleading statement (as only an "educated" infidel could), a quote by scientist: "Maybe there just wasn't enough room for them on the ark." The only redemptive quality of this sarcastic remark is that it is by far the most intelligent solution given by these darkened minds. II Timothy 3:7 points out that such men are "always learning and never able to come to the knowledge of the truth." The reason for their confusion is their refusal to accept the existence of the Author of Truth, God.

The biblical Flood explains the massive fossil record of dinosaurs found in the Earth, but doesn't account for the extinction of the dinosaurs that survived the Flood on the Ark. Creationists hold that a pair of each land creature was on the Ark, including dinosaurs, which couldn't have survived outside the vessel. What happened to the dinosaurs, and other creatures, that did come off the Ark but have somehow disappeared from the face of the Earth?

Chapter Thirty-Three

Why Dinosaurs Are Extinct: The Biblical Solution

The Second Law of Thermodynamics: The Curse.

Before we consider other possible solutions for the disappearance of dinosaurs, let us look at the second law of thermodynamics, which is described in the Bible as "the curse." This law states that everything is wearing out, growing old and dying. Thus, eventually all life would become extinct, according to this law, if it were not for God and His supernatural intervention.

Not only have the dinosaurs become extinct, but so have approximately 90 percent of all life forms (plants, animals, insects, birds, etc.). For example, within the past 350 years, almost 400 known species of major animal groupings have become extinct, and presently over 300 additional species are considered endangered — according to the environmentalists.

Man's selfishness — either his desire for sport or money or just plain ignorance — has led to the extinction or near extinction of certain species. The story of the American bison **(see fig. #159)** reveals this. At one time there were an estimated 50-100 million buffalo roaming the mid-west. Within a short, 10-year span during the 1800s, when they were hunted for sport and slaughtered wholesale, the numbers dropped to just a couple of thousand. Some reports state the number was as low as several hundred. Today, under the protection of the United States government, their numbers have once again increased to a safe level, but far from the original count.

The passenger pigeon **(see fig. #160)** is another example of a creature recently become extinct. During the 1800s, millions of them literally darkened the skies as they flew by in flocks. Passenger pigeons are gone now, and the body of the last bird to die has been stuffed and placed in the Smithsonian Institute in Washington, D.C.

On January 12, 1989, a documentary entitled "The Sinking Ark" was shown on public television. It examined the demise of many plants and animal species in wake of pollution, hunting and

Figure #159. THE BUFFALO: MAKING A COMEBACK

Figure #160. THE PASSING OF THE PASSENGER PIGEON

industrial development. Host Julian Pettifer noted that 20 years ago the Earth was losing one animal species per day. In other words, one species of animal, insect, bird, etc. was becoming extinct every day. Mr. Pettifer said the current statistics have changed somewhat. Instead of being one species per day, it now may be one an hour. Unless Christ returns, all life, not just the dinosaurs, will perish on the Earth — the inevitable consequence of sin.

Environmental Changes.

Environmental changes probably account for the extinction of many dinosaurs and other animals that came off the Ark after the Flood.

1. Weather Changes.

Until just recently, the sudden disappearance of dinosaurs has been a mystery to the evolutionist. However, evolutionists are continually looking for solutions, and the one previously discussed is now widely accepted. It is believed the Earth must have experienced a catastrophic event. This led to a drastic change in the weather, causing the quick extinction of many creatures and plants.

Interestingly, this theory harmonizes perfectly with the biblical revelation that the Earth has experienced numerous catastrophes affecting the entire globe. The granddaddy of them all was Noah's Flood. We read about it in Genesis 7:18-24:

> The waters rose and increased greatly on the earth, and the ark floated on the surface of the water. They rose greatly on the earth, and all the high mountains under the entire heavens were covered. The waters rose and covered the mountains to a depth of more than twenty feet. Every living thing that moved on the earth perished — birds, livestock, wild animals, all the creatures that swarm over the earth, and all mankind. Everything on dry land that had the breath of life in its nostrils died. Every living thing on the face of the earth was wiped out; men and animals and the creatures that move along the ground and the birds of the air were wiped from the earth. Only Noah was left, and those with him in the ark. The waters flooded the earth for a hundred and fifty days.

Those of us who believe the Bible to be true should expect that millions of fossils were buried in rock that was formed in water. That is exactly what can be found all around the globe — billions and billions of fossils found in rock which was formed in water. In fact, one particular deposit of shale rock in California contains a billion fish that died within a four-square-mile area.

The latest evolutionary theory about extinction suggests that some 65 million years ago, a meteorite hit the Earth's ocean and pierced through the floor, allowing volcanic material to be spewed into the stratosphere around the Earth. This led to a dramatic altering of the weather, then caused the abrupt extinction of the dinosaur.

The creationist would agree on the weather's changing, but would disagree on the fixing of the date: instead of 65 million years ago, it would be about 4,500 years ago, a date unthinkable among evolutionists.

According to the Creation Science account, the Flood and the Ice Age were simultaneous. After the Flood, the ice continued to exist in massive amounts around the poles; thus, weather patterns were considerably cooler all over the Earth. This cooling effect had a disastrous effect on the dinosaur community, being that they were reptilian and cold-blooded.

Reptiles cannot survive the cold except in a state of hibernation, and then only to a certain point.

They must maintain a temperature above freezing. They cannot exist for more than a few hours in freezing temperatures. Just three days of global sub-zero temperatures (below freezing), and all reptiles would quickly become extinct. Even an eclipse of the sun results in a temperature drop of several degrees in just a few moments.[36]

2. Food

Perhaps the lush, plenteous vegetation covering much of the Earth before the Flood was unavailable afterward. A fully-grown elephant can consume up to 450 pounds of vegetation daily. Some of the adult dinosaurs would have required several *thousand* pounds of food a day.

Many extinct species of tropical plants have been found in the rocks along with the dinosaurs, which is further indication that any atmospheric changes would not be conducive for survival. The few remaining dinosaurs were probably eventually killed by men hunting for food or who considered the creatures dangerous pests. Their numbers would have been considerably smaller after the Flood, making it fairly easy to eliminate them from the face of the Earth.

3. Atmospheric Pressure Differentiation.

One additional reason for the swift disappearance of the dinosaur is the absence of the water-vapor canopy which existed around the Earth before the Flood.[37] The loss of the canopy caused the atmospheric pressure to decrease about $1\frac{1}{4}$ times. This decrease helps to explain why these creatures would have had more and more difficulty breathing and moving about as they grew to massive proportions. The larger a creature, the greater the oxygen requirement to maintain proper metabolism. Before the Flood, when the dinosaurs flourished, there was more oxygen pressure per square inch, allowing for a greater oxygen intake through the nostrils, as well as by diffusion (absorption of oxygen into the skin). These giants do not exist today because they literally suffocated to death as they grew larger. The environmental conditions all over the Earth changed so drastically after the Flood, the dinosaurs simply could no longer survive in the "new world."

It must be remembered that because of sin, this whole world is doomed — all life is doomed — and some species will fall victim to the curse before others that are more adaptable and thus able to survive. It's like this world has a large sign posted on it: "Condemned. New Earth Under Construction." **(See fig. #161.)**

Figure #161. EARTH — CONDEMNED

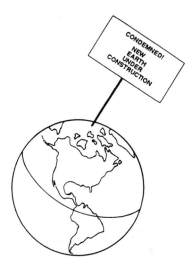

Chapter Thirty-Four

Gentle Giants or Blood-Thirsty Beasts?

Figure #162. BATTLE OF THE BEASTS

The Battle of the Gargantuans: Fact or Fiction?

Who hasn't seen a reptilian monster movie that included a battle to the finish between reptilian mega beasts "A" and "B," better known as T-rex and Tri-tops. **(See fig. #163.)** After watching that kind of movie, we walk away believing that these giant creatures were serial killers from birth. However, research is revealing a different story.

Hollywood has programmed us to believe that dinosaurs were mean and fierce — like King Kong, who roamed the world looking for cities such as Tokyo or New York to obliterate. However, these catastrophic caricatures are only the invention of the film producers' whimsical imaginations. They are not reality, and no one knows for sure just how dinosaurs behaved in real life.

Joke of a Park and Ludicrous World.

Most everyone has seen or heard about the blockbuster movie, *Jurassic Park*, and its sequel, *Lost World*. Both movies used the latest technological advances in computer animation to simulate dinosaurs, making them appear to be unbelievably real and very much alive. However, the plot and the portrayal of the dinosaurs' personalities, temperaments and natures are about as real as those of Puff

Figure #163. BATTLE OF THE GARGANTUANS

the Magic Dragon, Bugs Bunny and Wild E. Coyote. The movies should have been subtitled *Joke of a Park and Ludicrous World.*

The wizards of Hollywood, with inspiration from evolutionists and the almighty dollar, have beguiled the public into believing that the sharp teeth, claws and horns of some dinosaurs indicate they were ferocious creatures, roaming the land with killer instincts, attacking other creatures at random. Recent findings suggest this may not be the case at all.

Two Dogs, Two Dispositions.
(See figs. #164A & B.)

I have a relative who has two dogs. One is black and looks like the devil, yet it acts like an angel. It is as friendly as a man's best friend could be, yet it has the looks that only its mom could love. The other dog is white, cute and fluffy, but it acts like the devil incarnate. As long as visitors are around, it lets them know that it would just as soon eat them alive as look at them. I definitely keep my distance when I am visiting.

What is interesting is that you would never be able to tell their personalities by simply looking at their pictures. The dinosaurs have something in common with these two muts.

Figure #164A. THE ANGEL IN BLACK

Split Personality.

Believe it or not, T-rex may have had a side of its personality of which we are not aware. Now some scientists are stating that this may be the case with the fiercest of all the dinosaurs

Figure #164B. THE DEVIL IN WHITE

gargantuans. Of course, should someone attempt to steal its dinner, no doubt it could make sure that someone's day was ruined. But T-rex, the king of lizards, may in fact have been easy prey for "Fred Flintstone and company" (had they been living at the same time and in the same country). In other words T-rex most likely couldn't have lived up to the fierce image portrayed in *Jurassic Park* and *Lost World*. Its bark may have been far worse than its bite.

Were Dinosaurs Ferocious?

Furthermore, to diminish T-rex's ferocious reputation even more, its dagger-like teeth wouldn't have remained intact if it fought with another mega beast. Research has revealed that they were not well rooted. **(See fig. #165.)** The roots of their teeth had knobs rather than hooks like the roots of human teeth do. In addition, studies have discovered that the edges of their

Figure #165. TAKING A LOOK AT T-REX'S FRAGILE TEETH

teeth were serrated, kind of like the teeth on a saw. Traces of chlorophyll, the green material found in plants, have been found embedded on their teeth. This means that their teeth may not have been used for crunching and crushing bones, but for cutting and sawing tough grasses, canes and stalks.

For those who think of the T-rex as vicious, there is an additional problem; it's in the anatomy of its front legs. Either these legs were the result of some genetic miscue or they were never intended for fighting. They appear too fragile for seizing and clutching struggling prey, and are too short to reach its mouth in the event it decided to eat its catch. **(See fig. #166.)**

With all of these obstacles, how is it that Mr. T-rex has become known as the most frightening of all the dinosaurs? T-rex could have had a horrifying appearance that only its mother could love, like a host of other totally ugly critters — my relative's dog, for instance. But that doesn't mean it was ferocious. That is simply Hollywood hoopla. The film industry has a strange fascination with blood, teeth, jaws, claws and other butchering devices that can easily make mincemeat out of a person's anatomical parts.

Not only were the T-rex's teeth not well rooted, which would have caused many to be left behind if

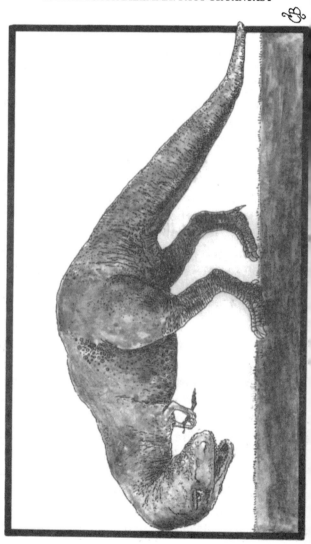

Figure #166. NATURE'S MISCUE? T-REX'S FOREARMS

it feasted on a Triceratops for dinner as Hollywood portrays, but it would have made them easy prey for humans to hunt, trap and even kill.

The Bigger They Are, the Harder They Fall. (See fig. #167.)

Most everyone has watched a cartoon where a "Gigantasaurus" is pursuing a small critter, only to trip and plunge head over heals, shaking the Earth while receiving a baseball-sized knot on its noggin. But the anatomy of the Tyranno-saurus rex indicates that it most likely moved extremely slow and even waddled like a duck. As a result, most other creatures, including other dinosaurs, would have easily escaped in a foot race.

James Furlough of Purdue University, who is an expert in dinosaur demolition, tells us that T-rex could have been tripped easily in a fast pursuit, and could have crashed head first into the ground, smashing into a lifeless heap. Even the tail of a massive, non-violent vegetarian dinosaur like Apatosaurus could cause T-rex to trip by simply swinging its tail around into the path of T-rex as it galloped by.

Furlough reasons that T-rex was so heavy and tall that if it were to fall in a chase, its weight would literally slam it into the ground at an

Figure #167. THE BIGGER THEY ARE, THE HARDER THEY FALL

acceleration of six 'Gs — or six times the pull of gravity. Such a fall would dismember its tiny front legs, and the impact on its brain would have required a barrel full of aspirin to relieve the headache it would have had when it revived. Imagine having a sudden fall while running at full speed. And instead of having arms, hands and fingers to break your fall, you only have tiny fingers. Do you get the picture? If your entire weight were to land on your fingers, no doubt the pain would bring tears to your eyes. It is unlikely that such huge creatures were fast movers simply because it wasn't in their best interest. The danger of stumbling was too great. If a T-rex fell and entered a comatose state, hunters could finish it off and slice up enough meat for a lot of T-rex burgers.

Since the Tyrannosaurs were easy prey, it could be that men who were hunters helped to kill them off after the Flood. Man's intelligence was and always has been, more dreadful than any animal's size or strength, including that of King Kong.

Chapter Thirty-Five

Were Dinosaurs Meat Eaters?

(See fig. #168.)

Veggie Eaters at the Beginning.

The Bible reveals that Adam and his family were meant to enjoy all of the animals and to rule over them in kindness. In the beginning, all animals were friendly; and none of them ate meat or killed other creatures for food. God provided enough plants for both man and animals to eat. Man had not yet sinned, and there was no death, disease, or evil anywhere on Earth. Everything was perfect — until sin came.

> Therefore, just as sin entered the world through one man, and death through sin, and in this way death came to all men, because all sinned (Rom. 5:12).

A Taste for "Blood."

Today, numerous animals kill other animals for food. And there is something sinister about

Figure #168. MR. GROUCH

many of the ways in which animals get their food. It is as though we are witnessing the direct effects of sin. Thorns and thistles, blood-sucking parasites, disease-producing bacteria, and fighting to the death are common in the animal world. Exactly when these "evil" traits began to surface is not known, but they probably started soon after man's first sin.

As a result of Adam and Eve's sin in the Garden, the creation was cursed. Thorns, disease, death and decay became a sad but common, everyday reality, even in the animal world as they struggled to survive. Before man sinned, all the animals ate plants, not meat (Gen. 1:30). It was not until after man's rebellion that animals began to eat other animals. Nowhere in Scripture is there any indication that animals were violent meat eaters until after Noah's Flood. Instead, the Bible reveals that it was mankind that was first to be wicked and perverted. Remember, Adam and Eve's first offspring, Cain, murdered his own brother.

When the animals came off the Ark following the Flood, the world and its environment had drastically changed. At that time, God gave mankind formal approval to slay animals for food (Gen. 9:2,3). Humans, however, were never to be slain; the man or the animal who did so was to pay with his own life: "Whoever sheds the blood of man, by man shall his blood be shed" (Gen. 9:5).

God caused a fear and dread of man to "fall upon all the beasts of the earth and all the birds of the air, upon every creature that moves along the ground, and upon all the fish of the sea" (Gen. 9:2).

"Be Continually Filled."

Be filled with the Spirit (Eph. 5:18).

Since Jesus' life, death and resurrection, Christians have an antidote to the negative effects of sin and the curse. The Apostle Paul admonishes us to be filled with the Spirit of the Living God. In the original Greek language, this verse actually directs us to be filled continually, meaning it is an ongoing, never-ending undertaking.

It is imperative that we are filled with and led by the Spirit of God. One reason this is so important is that from time to time we hear of someone who is attacked and killed by an animal. It may have been the result of carelessness, etc. Or possibly it was an attack from Satan, in which he empowered or influenced the animal to strike. Satan does have the power to enter the animal kingdom (see Gen. 3, Mk. 5). But the believer in Christ has been given authority over all the powers of darkness, as well as nature. However, if we are careless or ignorant of such authority or fail to exercise it, we will suffer. Because the world is tainted by sin, we are not free to walk through a jungle (including our inner-city, concrete jungles) without taking caution. Being led by the Spirit will keep us from suffering unnecessarily by being in the wrong place at the wrong time.

Post-Flood Changes.

It is very possible that after the Flood animals developed characteristics for surviving in their new environment. It became necessary for some of them to attack and kill for food to support and sustain their own lives and keep the species from becoming extinct. Even humans, when experiencing hunger pains, are inclined to insensitivity, irritability, anger and a host of other negative characteristics, until they satisfy their hunger.

The pre-Flood Earth with its luxuriant vegetation and uniform temperatures worldwide, was a conducive environment for a comfortable, tranquil and sedate lifestyle, both for humans and for the animal kingdom. A peaceable temperament can be simulated today, even among the normally more aggressive animals such as lions and tigers. Animal trainers have trained carnivorous animals and other wild creatures to be tame, even docile. One key to keeping them docile is feeding them well, so that hunger pains are minimal. Neutering the animal's reproductive system also diminishes the instinctive tendencies in the more aggressive animals.

During Noah's Flood, the world was devastated. Much of the rich, fertile soil was washed into the oceans. Afterwards, radiation levels became much higher. Food was no longer abundant. All this may have instigated changes in the order of provision in nature so that the remaining species could survive.

Forming Habits.

Animals form habits, either through following their instincts or as a result of trial and error. Some creatures acquire a taste for certain things, which can result in some very bad habits.

Let's say you're sitting in your living room watching television and eating popcorn. Your dog looks up at you with longing eyes as if to say, "Just one kernel, please." You're in a generous mood, so you share one kernel with this sweet little dog. Of course, he wants more, but you firmly say, "No!" Later, as you're going off to bed, you dump a few remaining kernels in the garbage. The next morning, to your surprise, your obedient little dog has turned over the trash and spread it everywhere to find those kernels. You can be sure that your dog has developed a taste for popcorn — and whatever else he found to eat in the trash.

Some of the worst problems arise when an animal develops a taste for blood. Perhaps it was because of this taste for blood that sinister habits began to become more prevalent among the more aggressive animals. Not all of animals' habits are detrimental. Today, animals do help maintain a clean and balanced environment. Many animals are scavengers and help to remove dead and decaying carcasses; otherwise bacteria, disease and plagues could ravage the entire planet, as they have in isolated areas.

Since the Flood, both humans and animals need a diet fortified with protein, which meat supplies, in order to strengthen and sustain their bodies. What terrible and awesome consequences sin had on God's original paradise! As the Apostle Paul said, "The whole creation has been groaning as in the pains of childbirth right up to the present time" (Rom. 8:22).

Chapter Thirty-Six

Resolving T-Rex's Split Personality

Buzzard Mentality.

Suppose Tyrannosaurus rex *was* a meat eater. This doesn't necessarily make it ferocious. It may have been a scavenger, like a buzzard. And there are numerous creatures that have very sharp teeth, but are total vegetarians or only rarely eat flesh. Size is not necessarily a factor. There are myriads of creatures with claws and sharp teeth or beaks, yet quite timid by nature such as the vulture and even the hyena when it is alone. The beaver **(see fig. #169)** has sharp teeth, but it does not use them for ripping flesh; it uses them for chewing through the tough trunks of trees.

There are many other mild-mannered animals with extremely sharp teeth, such as apes and gorillas. Gorillas **(see fig. #170)** have very fierce looking teeth, and yet they don't eat meat. The

Figure #169. THE BEAVER

Figure #170. THE APE

giant panda **(see fig. #171)** of China and the fruit bat of Australia both have teeth that will slice through a tough Texas steak, and yet they don't eat Texas steaks — or any meat at all. The panda's sharp teeth are only for slicing through thick and hard bamboo shoots.

Because some of the dinosaurs had claws does not necessarily mean they were used for tearing into prey; they may have been used for gathering food and holding it while they ate. No one alive today ever lived with a dinosaur; therefore, no one can be sure of their natures and temperaments. Remember, Hollywood is full of hoopla.

Signs of Mild-Manneredness.

Another indication these large creatures may not have been as ferocious as the movies have made them out to be is the discovery of some of their fossilized teeth. The teeth show little or no wear. Some of the teeth had fragile and delicate edges **(see fig. #172)**, yet were preserved almost in flawless condition. These features indicate that they were not used to rip muscle or crunch bones, vertebrae and other solid material. Instead, they were used on pulpy and softer substances, like foliage.

It is entirely possible that some of the larger

Figure #171. THE PANDA

Figure #172. NATURE'S BUTCHER KNIFE

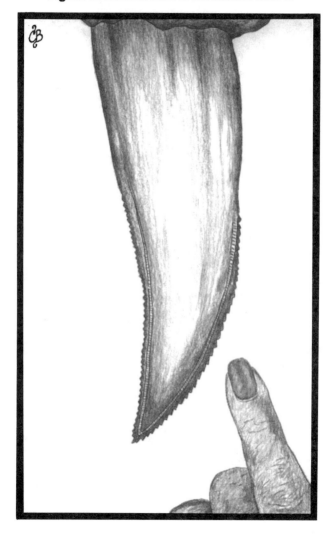

dinosaurs that have been perceived to be ferocious were only plant and fruit eaters, and not carnivorous at all. Just as the shape of a knife does not indicate what it is used for, it is the same with the shape of teeth. Teeth have different uses, and their shape cannot be conclusive evidence as to their purpose. Nor does the shape indicate what food they chewed on. Sharp teeth can serve purposes other than tearing meat, just as kitchen knives can be used to cut carrots, celery and other hard vegetables rather than on meat.

Peacock Paraphernalia.

Another sign that testifies that dinosaurs did not live up to their fierce image is that ferocious carnivorous animals are generally very sleek — like the cheetah, jaguar and tiger. Their anatomy isn't delicate, with fragile parts such as crests or plumage which could be easily cracked or broken. These would only get in their way, causing them difficulties during a battle or while on the run.

Some of the reptilian creatures had fragile spines connected to their backs over six feet high, which stood straight up in the air. **(See fig. #173.)** Any kind of a life-and-death struggle, or even wrestling just for play, could result in damage to these delicate parts. Triceratops and

Figure #173. FRAGILE SPINES

Stegosaurus and others had bony spikes and plates on their heads, backs or tails. God did not necessarily create these features for battle. There are other reasons for such paraphernalia. Many creatures today have unique characteristics, like peacocks have plumage to attract mates or scare away predators. So there could be any number of reasons for the horns, spikes and bony plates on certain dinosaurs. For instance, horns can be used to plow and dig for food where there is thick undergrowth and rotting logs. The powerful

Figure #174. RHINO BETTLE

jaws, teeth and horns of Triceratops may have been used to pierce tough roots and limbs in order to get to grubs and for softening tough tree trunks before chewing them.

Have you ever seen a rhinoceros beetle? **(See fig. #174.)** Like a number of insects, the rhinoceros beetle has horns somewhat like those of certain dinosaurs — smaller of course, yet enormous in comparison to their bodies. In the past, scientists thought that these horns were used for fighting with and injuring other beetles. However, it has been learned that the horns are primarily used for lifting and prying small twigs, etc. to find small insects to eat.

Chapter Thirty-Seven

The Effects of Sin

The Whole World Became Corrupt.

God originally commanded Adam and Eve and the animals to eat only plants. For Adam and Eve, there was one exception — they were not to eat the fruit of the tree of knowledge of good and evil. They deliberately disobeyed, and as a result of their sin, rebellion and violence entered the world. Adam and Eve's very first child, Cain, became a murderer, and all of their descendants disobeyed God. The whole world became corrupted. No doubt even animals were subject to the effects of sin, and they began preying on other animals. Just as thorns and thistles began to grow as a result of the curse, dagger-like teeth, horns, spikes and razor-sharp claws may also have been a result of the curse.

It is likely that God rescued the creatures of the world from quick destruction by preparing them with defensive weapons to help protect them from aggressive creatures, including self-centered man. Perhaps such defensive mechanisms and weapons were not enough. For man became so evil and violent that God had to send a worldwide Flood to wipe the evil off of the face of the Earth.

> The LORD saw how great man's wickedness on the earth had become, and that every inclination of the thoughts of his heart was only evil all the time (Gen 6:5).

Who knows, maybe before the Flood even came many animal species were already extinct or were near extinction because of man's abusive and exploitive ways.

As a result of the Flood, Earth's environment dramatically changed. Much of the world became hostile toward life. The life span of man was drastically shortened — by 900 percent — to retard his bent to sin.

Whether dinosaurs were as ferocious as we have been led to believe will no doubt continue to be a mystery. However, the Bible tells us that all creatures were created with a purpose, which included calm and tranquil temperaments, for they all lived peacefully with each other until sin entered the picture. Someday God will restore

His creation to be a paradise where all creatures, including man, will live in peace, and the whole world will be filled with the knowledge of his love.

> For the earth will be filled with the
> knowledge of the glory of the LORD,
> as the waters cover the sea (Hab. 2:14).

Chapter Thirty-Eight

Peace on Earth, Good Will Toward Men and Dinosaurs

(See fig. #175.)

Peaceful Dragons.

In the beginning, dinosaurs were peaceful. T-rex was just an overgrown Teddysaurus. Today they have become symbols of dragons. What happened? What went wrong? To understand the problem in depth, we need to look back before the dinosaurs were created. We need to look all the way back at love *before* first sight.

God is the Lover of Our Souls.

God loved people before He ever created them. There was peace on Earth among all the creatures God had made, including the dinosaurs. Man was not created until the end of the sixth day. God created man for His pleasure. In other words, He has an enormous reservoir of love within His great being that desires an object upon which to focus. That object is man. Human beings are the most complex and beautiful of all God's creations, and He desires a mutual, intimate relationship of love with us. This is a mystery beyond comprehension to the natural man; it takes an incredible revelation to understand this.

The book of the Song of Solomon has both a natural and a spiritual application. It is a book that expresses the love of a bridegroom and his bride. It describes the joy of freely expressed love. Through the spiritual interpretation, God reveals His intense passion — an ardent affection — for mankind. God is in love with mankind, but often we do not reciprocate His love. What does this great love have to do with dinosaurs? Read on. You will realize that dinosaurs were created partly as a result of God's love for man.

Satan will do anything he can to wound a person so that he/she will not be able to receive the loving advances of God because of feelings of being unwanted and rejected. One of the greatest hindrances to romantic love is one of the partners having no sense of their own attractiveness. God says, "I have stretched out my hands all day long to a rebellious people." (Isa. 65:2). When a person wakes each morning, God is anticipating intimate fellowship with him, but is

Figure #175. PEACEFUL DRAGONS

usually disappointed. Even Christians rarely have intimate fellowship with God. Some change their tone of voice when they pray, thinking this is intimate fellowship. It is only a religious pretense — far from an intimate relationship.

Man: The Beautiful Handiwork of God.

Every human being is the beautiful handiwork of God. Just how beautiful and unique are we? There has never been a person like you or me before, and there will never be one again. Every person is totally unique, one of a kind. The mold, the pattern, was thrown away after God created you.

What makes a one of a kind in art, clothing, sculpture or jewelry so valuable and desirable? Because it is the only one of its kind in all of the universe. Likewise, this uniqueness of every person is valuable to God. Each one of us has the potential to reveal certain aspects of Christ's character never before revealed on this planet. That is how unique every person is.

So when we see a bedraggled skid-row bum or a totally depraved transvestite, we must realize they are a paradox. They are fallen human beings; but if they would accept God's loving advances and turn from their wickedness, they have the potential of becoming a vessel of honor and revealing Jesus in a way that no other being can or ever will. This is true with every person, no matter what their race, nation or culture. Every person has the potential of bringing God incredible pleasure by expressing love to Him. God's passion for His bride is unabated. He has the same ardent love for every man and woman, boy and girl He did when He created Adam and Eve.

Misconceptions of God's Love.

God's love toward people never ceases, even though people's love toward Him is sadly lacking or even nonexistent. But if mankind is fallen — sinful, meaning our sins have separated us from this holy, righteous God, can we enter into close fellowship with Him? Let's say I went camping with my wife. I warned her there was a swamp nearby, but she failed to heed my warning and fell into the swamp and became covered with muck and mire. Would I dismiss her from being my wife if I love her? Or would I seek instead to clean her up? God sees us as beautiful, but covered with mud. Through Jesus Christ, He offers us the opportunity to clean up.

Another traditional misconception has taught that because of sin, God is extremely wrathful and to be feared. After all, wasn't the God of the Old Testament full of wrath and vengeance? But He's the same God of the New Testament, Who is revealed as full of love and mercy. God is never changing. He was loving and merciful in Old Testament times, and He's tough regarding sin and rebellion in New Testament times.

Because of their misconceptions about God's nature, people have come up with the notion that God's wrath can be appeased by gifts, even blood and human sacrifices — or at least by suffering. Thus out of fear, man has attempted to worship God by abusing himself with rituals of self-in-flicted torment. However, it was not the love of God that needed to be restored by the death of Christ because it was never lost. The death of Christ was to satisfy a legal requirement. God's ultimate objective in the atoning death of Christ was not just to rescue souls from hell, but to restore a ruptured relationship.

Jesus came to this earth to "save that which was lost" (Matt. 18:11 NKJV). What was lost? The intimate relationship between God and man in the Garden. Jesus came to reveal and to heal the broken heart of the Father. He came to make a way for peace to reign again on planet Earth.

At this point, you are probably thinking that we are a million miles from the subject of dinosaurs. So let's look at how this fits into the picture. Once we understand the reason why God created us and that He still desires to restore that broken relationship, then we can see God created the dinosaurs in the first place.

Wedding Bells.

When God created the world, it was to be a wedding present for humans. He carpeted the world with incredibly beautiful meadows, bubbling springs, rolling hills and majestic mountains. Then He surrounded it with a universe filled with stars. Everything — even the landscape under the sea — had awesome color, design and beauty. The lush vegetation of trees, ferns, plants and flowers came in an infinite number of shapes, colors, designs and scents, which revealed the amorous nature of God. There were mammals, birds, fish and incredible mechanisms within the insect world — all alive with color, sound and motion. God was getting ready for a wedding.

What was the excitement within the heart of God that caused Him to burst forth with such creativity? It was the anticipation of a relationship with an incredibly beautiful creature who was still in His imagination. Finally, He created the epitome of what was beautiful and desirable to Him. And just what did this creature look like? He looks like every son of Adam, and she looks like every daughter of Eve. Creation was to be a wedding present to the creatures God wanted to marry. This is still His plan. The wedding has been postponed, but it is very near. It will be the wedding of all weddings, the wedding of His Son to His bride — redeemed man. Next time, however, the wedding present will surely surpass the original. But, first peace had to be re-established between God and man.

Dinosaurs: Part of the Original Wedding Present.

Creation included the dinosaur family. Like all of the other creatures God created, He brought the dinosaurs to Adam to see what he would name them. They were to be man's friends and helpers.

There are many animals that are useful to man today. No doubt before the rebellion and the subsequent curse, God's plan was that all creatures would be friendly and useful to man. Maybe the dinosaur family could have been as useful to man, just as the ox, camel, elephants and others are today. Is it too improbable to imagine that the dinosaurs may have been designed by God to be used in place of today's modern machinery? The curse has had devastating effects upon life on planet Earth, causing changes in the nature of animals so they could survive. But God's plans may have been almost too incredible for us to believe.

Imagine for a moment that the creatures of the dinosaur kingdom were created to provide man with some kind of useful service. There are creatures today that sometimes exhibit a diabolical and powerful side, but can also display a tender and gentle side. For instance, the crocodile can crush the bones of a wilderbeast caught in its jaws, then use those same jaws to pick up its tiny fragile newly-hatched young and carry them to safety.

Could the giant beasts of the past have had some delicate and sensitive qualities in God's original plan and purpose? Could some of the larger creatures — such as the Apatosaurus, Diplodocus, and Brachiosaurus have been trained to do heavy construction or farm work such as moving steel I-beams, pallets of brick and lumber, or hauling wagons of hay? **(See fig. #176.)** Hundreds of millions of dollars are spent each year on equipment to move things and construct buildings. I know all this sounds a bit like science fiction, yet the Bible tells us that God made man to rule over the animals.

Figure #176. DINO-MIGHT

Then God said, "Let us make man in our image, in our likeness, and let them rule over the fish of the sea and the birds of the air, over the livestock, over all the earth, and over all the creatures (dinosaurs) that move along the ground" (Gen. 1:26).

To rule means to command, control, direct, guide and dictate to. When Adam was asked to name the animals, he must have had an understanding of their abilities, capabilities, and skills and no doubt named them according to their nature, character, disposition and temperament.

Chapter Thirty-Nine

The Great Dinosaur Adventure

The World of Dinotopia.

Let's take a journey to the land that never was, but was supposed to be. Envision yourself a teenager, and you and several of your friends are taking a camping trip to the Grand Canyon in Arizona. After arriving, you look for a place to set up camp, but last week's destructive storms have messed up the camping sight.

The park ranger calls for assistance, and heavy-duty "equipment" quickly arrives to take care of the fallen trees and other debris. The "equipment" is a group of trained dinosaurs. Triceratops helps to uproot some tree trunks with its massive weight and horns. T-rex assists by crunching branches with its bone-crushing teeth, making them into kindling. Apatosaurus drags off the trunks of trees. And a team of Diplodocuses devour several tons of vegetation for their afternoon snack. Later, a herd of Seismosauruses arrive to help smooth out the ground with their huge steam-rolling bodies and tails. **(See fig. #177.)**

After setting up the tents, it is time for dinner. Unfortunately, the pile of logs is still damp from the recent heavy rains. But there just happens to be a neighborly leviathan nearby, and it assists you in starting the fire with one blazing blast from its mouth. **(See fig. #178.)** Finally, everyone settles in for a good night's rest.

The next morning the group is awed at the inspiring view from the rim of the canyon. The camp director informs everyone that they will be taking an aerial ride to see the canyon from above. The flight will not be in a helicopter, but a "dragoncopter." The park has a flock of trained Pterodactyls, and each can carry a sightseer. What a ride. **(See fig. #179.)**

After being safely dropped off at the bottom of the canyon, everyone takes a journey down the Colorado river — not in a raft, but on the back of an Ultrasaurus. Even the raging river doesn't seem to hamper or frighten the behemoth.

> When the river rages, he is not alarmed; he is secure, though the Jordan should surge against his mouth (Job 40:23).

Figure #177. CALLING 911-DINO

Figure #178. GOT A MATCH?

Figure #179. DRAGONCOPTERS

Everyone is safe, high above the water. **(See fig. #180.)** When the journey brings the group to a calmer portion of the river, you and your friends go for a swim, and you all use the head of the creature as a diving platform. Each kid gets the Utrasaurus to lower or raise its head to the desirable height. For the fearless, 50 feet is the maximum. It's an experience which catapults them upward through the air for a rush they won't forget. **(See fig. #181.)**

Is Anything Too Hard for God?

Does all this sound like a whimsical fairy tale, a ride at Disneyland, or just plain old nonsense? The real question is, how big is your God? Is anything to hard for Him? No one knows what life on this planet would have been like had man not rebelled in the Garden. But Adam and Eve did rebel. Now God is planning a new creation that will far exceed the original one. What we have today is but a decaying remnant of the original.

Loving fathers enjoy giving their children gifts that provide special moments to remember. But with a disobedient child, a father sometimes must withhold the gifts he planned to give lest he reinforce the rebellious attitude. So it has been with the Creator of the universe. He has so much

Figure #180. RAFTING WAS NEVER LIKE THIS

Figure #181. SWIMMING WITH THE BIG BOYS

to offer man, but He can't because it would only reinforce man's irresponsible behavior. However, there is a day coming when the present heavens and Earth will pass away:

> By the same word the present heavens and earth are reserved for fire, being kept for the day of judgment and destruction of ungodly men (II Pet. 3:7).

God is in the process of creating a totally new and awesome world that words cannot explain.

> I know a man in Christ who ... was caught up to paradise. ... He heard inexpressible things, things that man is not permitted to tell (II Cor. 12:2-4).

> But in keeping with his promise we are looking forward to a new heaven and a new earth, the home of righteousness (II Pet. 3:13).

> So then, dear friends, since you are looking forward to this, make every effort to be found spotless, blameless and at peace with him (II Pet. 3:14).

That day will include a celebration that will make the fantastically beautiful New Year's

Rose Parade and Disneyland's Electric Parade fade in its glory. Who knows, there may even be dinosaurs in the procession! **(See fig. #182.)**

Peace on Earth.

When Christ came to Earth the first time, God sent angels to provide an incredible birth announcement to the shepherds.

> Glory to God in the highest, and on earth peace among men with whom He is pleased! (Lk. 2:14 RSV).

When Christ arrives the second time, He will establish His Kingdom throughout the entire universe. There will be peace and good will — both to man and to all the creatures, even to dinosaurs — those terrible lizards of old.

> The kingdom of the world has become the kingdom of our Lord and of his Christ, and he will reign for ever and ever (Rev. 11:15).

Figure #182. NEW YEAR'S DAY PARADE

Chapter Forty

Birdosaur

(See fig. 183.)

"Living Dinosaurs Found in Cuba."

As we draw near to the end of our adventures in the kingdom of the dinosaurs, there is one more aspect we must not overlook. It involves another evolutionary tale about a creature that grew feathers overnight. The story begins in Cuba with this opening stanza:

> Once upon a time there lived a bee that was a bird who was told he was a cousin of a dinosaur. The Mellisuga Helenae is only $2\frac{1}{4}$ inches long, and is found only in Cuba. Can you believe that this tiny bee hummingbird **(see fig. #184)** is actually the smallest dinosaur in the world?

This is what a recent publication from the Museum of Natural History in New York City

Figure #183. BIRDOSAUR

Figure #184. "HI, CUZ!"

Bee Hummingbird

declares. Some evolutionists are claiming it is true. Sound ridiculous?

You must understand that evolutionists are so determined to prove that birds are descendants of dinosaurs that they will continue to come up with all kinds of incredible possibilities in hopes of supporting their theory.

Birdolink.

Time magazine (April 1993) featured a cover story of a reptile-like creature with feathers that supposedly was a transitional link between dinosaurs and birds. However, the writer of the article actually admitted that the creature did not in fact have feathers.

Yet evolutionists are certain that birds are descendants of dinosaurs and are bent on finding the missing "birdosaur" link. They make all sorts of incredible claims to persuade the public.

They try to infiltrate our minds with their godless ideas, often in very subtle ways, For instance, at the beginning of the movie *Lost World*, a little girl sees some dinosaurs and asks whether or not they were little birds.

We must stay on guard against these insidious attacks. Remember, frogs can literally be boiled to death without realizing what is happening. When the changes in their environment are so slow and subtle that they do not detect the increase in temperature, they are killed by the boiling water, though they could have easily leaped to safety if they had been more cautious.

Likewise, many Christians do not realize the subtle indoctrination of evolutionary humanism which has slowly influenced their belief system. Instead of holding fast to the creation story of the Bible, some Christians succumb to the slow seduction of the humanistic evolutionists, who teach absurd ideas, such as man is the product of blind chance and dinosaurs evolved into birds.

Chapter Forty-One

The Missing Chain

Transitional Forms.

We don't hear much about "missing links" these days as it is much more in vogue to refer to them as "transitional forms." The new name does not call attention to the fact that these forms exist only in the minds of the evolutionists. There are not only missing links, but there is an entire missing chain.

Suppose an American visiting the magnificent Great Wall of China (2,000 miles in length) tells a Chinese person that America is in the process of finishing a chain link fence that will stretch clear across America from Los Angeles to New York City (3,000 miles). But when the American shows the Chinese person pictures of the fence, he quickly recognizes that there are only a couple of short links completed — one in New York and one in Los Angeles and concludes that the boastful American is stretching the truth.

That is the scenario with the evolutionary theory. There are millions and millions of missing links.

Students are taught in many colleges and universities that there is abundance of fossil evidence which reveals gradual transformations from fish to amphibians, amphibians to reptiles, reptiles to mammals, and so on. Evolutionary textbooks convincingly illustrate what these intermediate forms supposedly looked like. However, we must remember to ask the question: "What is the evidence?" In actuality, there are no clear fossil transitions between any of the above groups — only ideas. The pictures in the textbook are artistic conceptions of what these transitions might have looked like — if they had existed! Evolutionists all over the world are searching for such links in the layers of the Earth's strata, but 100 years of probing has produced absolutely nothing.

What is the Evidence?

It is crucial when looking at fossils to consider the manner of fossil reconstruction and to ask on what evidence the fossil is based. Many times the evidence is extremely scant, and the fossil is based almost is entirely on evolutionary bias.

The problem is that these artistic reconstructions are convincing to the college student who is unaware that they are created according to evolutionary preconceived ideas than on actual evidence. Plus, his or her class grade often depends upon the acceptance of these evolutionary views as fact. Most students never stop to ask the question, "What is the evidence?" They tend to accept it as fact because they saw it in a book, magazine or museum. And besides, the professor has a Ph.D. in science. So that is enough to convince most of the unwary public, that such a theory must indeed be factual. What is the evidence for the birdolink?

Chapter Forty-Two

Archaeopteryx: A Case of Fossil Foolery

The Rest of the Story
(See fig. #185.)

Archaeopteryx: A Transitional Link?

The remains of an ancient bird, which had been caught in flooded silt and preserved, have been called Archaeopteryx (pronounced ark-a-op-ter-ix). **(See fig. #186.)** For years it has been proposed as a link between reptiles and birds, as it appears to have both reptilian and bird characteristics.

If evolutionism were true, all kinds of transitional links should have been found by now. But never has there been found a fossil of a fish that emerged from the water and became an amphibian, not to mention a dinosaur becoming a bird. Nevertheless, there are plenty of pictures of such evolving creatures in films and books of evolutionists, though not one iota of evidence has ever been found. Some evolutionists have tried to

Figure #185. THE SORE FOLLY OF
MISS POLLYSAUR

Figure #186. ARCHAEOPTERYX: THE EVOLUTIONARY WISHBONE

refer to the oriental mudskipper **(see fig. #187)** as proof; however, keep in mind that it is still fully a fish, no matter what fantasy is concocted about its past.

How Ancient is the "Ancient Wing"?

In 1861, fossils of a creature were found in Germany. It was named Archaeopteryx, which means "ancient wing." The creature had claws on its wings, teeth in its mouth, and a bony tail. It also had wings and feathers.

Because this pigeon-size bird had some "reptile-like" characteristics, evolutionists claimed it is a "link" between birds and reptiles. Thus, there have been many books written and television programs produced declaring that Archaeopteryx is indeed a link between the reptile and the bird.

Are the teeth and claws on this creature any proof that it is a link, that is part bird and part reptile? Not at all. Some birds, such as the ostrich, have claws on their wings. Some have teeth or tooth-like projections. The fact that an extinct bird had teeth or claws says nothing of its ancestral connections to reptiles.

Besides the ostrich, the hoatzin of South America, the touraco of Africa, the rhea, and sometimes the adult gallinaceous birds all have

Figure #187. MUDSKIPPER

claws or claw-like appendages. If these birds were now extinct and their fossils were found today, they would undoubtedly be called missing links by evolutionists.

Some Have Teeth and Some Don't.

Just because Archaeopteryx had teeth is no indication that it is a missing link. It just so happens that some birds have teeth and some do not. Likewise, some reptiles have teeth and some do not, like turtles. Even some fish have teeth, and some do not. There are some mammals that have teeth, but some do not, as well as some humans who have teeth and some who do not. Although we might like to believe that certain irritating and unfriendly humans are a link between man and baboon, they are not!

Why do evolutionists feel so strongly about this creature being a link? People generally believe that scientists have formulated their ideas from the evidence. However, scientists are no different than anyone else. They have an underlying worldview that colors the way they interpret the evidence.

The fact of the matter is that Archaeopteryx is simply a bird. It has perching feet and was fully feathered like any other bird. No creatures on Earth have feathers except birds. And yet, according to the evolutionists, reptiles somehow converted their scales into feathers. A scale is nothing but a fold on the skin. So how in the world did folds on the skin of a lizard evolve into the intricate design of a feather?

To make matters worse — for the evolutionists, that is — never has anything been found in the fossil record of an intermediate form between the fold in the reptiles' skin and the feather of a bird.

Chapter Forty-Three

Feathers: The Trademark of the Bird

Models of Remarkable Engineering.
(See fig. #188.)

Feathers are an example of an amazing feat of complex engineering. They have a central shaft with a series of crisscross barbs extending out on each side, much like a chain link fence. The crisscross barbs have tiny hooks on them which lock them into place to form a mesh. **(See fig. #189.)** They are so tiny they can't be seen with the naked eye. If the mesh comes unhooked at any point, the bird simply runs his beak through its feathers, and the hooks relatch much like a zipper. An eagle's feathers are held together by more than 250,000 tiny hooks, and there are more than 7,000 feathers covering its body, yet all 7,000 weigh only about 21 ounces.

Feathers combine several marvelous quali-

Figure #188. FEATHERS

Figure #189. BARBS AND HOOKS

ties: lightness, strength and flexibility. They protect the bird's sensitive skin and act as an insulator so efficient that they keep a bird's temperature at the normal 107.7 degrees F. even in subfreezing weather.

A bird is a model of efficiency, combining low weight and great strength. They are an amazing model of aerodynamic perfection, making airplane designers envious. Volumes could be written on the many other wonderful features birds have, which reveals evidence of an all-knowing

Designer rather than the unintelligent cosmic forces of time, matter and chance which evolutionism declares as the creator.

The fossil record reveals that birds and their feathers appeared suddenly and were fully developed. There is no evidence of primitive feathers evolving. The idea that feathers evolved from frayed out scales is nothing but pure 21st century fantasy.

A Mélange?

No doubt Archaeopteryx is a mosaic created by God completely and fully developed. Its unusual characteristics make it distinctive.

Mélange means "mixture." Scientists refer to an animal which has traits similar to other animals, but are not related to those other animals, as mélanges. For example, the Australian platypus **(see fig. #77)** is a living example of an animal, like the fossil Archaeopteryx, that has a mixture of traits that are seen in other animals. It has a bill like a duck, yet it didn't come from a duck; it lays eggs like a reptile, yet it isn't evolving into a reptile. It has a tail like a beaver, yet it isn't related to the beaver. It uses sound and echo-location to find food, like a bat, but no one expects it to fly in the near future. The little platypus is a uniquely and distinctively, created animal which has adapted quite successfully to life in Australia. Maybe Archaeopteryx is also a mélange?

Chapter Forty-Four

Escaping to New Heights of "Reason"

Or How to Jump Across the Grand Canyon
(See fig. #190.)

An Adult Fairy Tale.

The evolutionary pipe dream about bir-dosaurs gets even more amazing. *The 1980 Science Yearbook* featured an evolutionary view of how birds' ancestors learned to climb trees to catch their breakfast. The article explained that the ancestors of birds learned to climb trees to escape from predators and to seek insect food. Once the "pre-bird" creature began dwelling in trees, feathers and wings evolved to aid in guiding it from branch to branch. And according to some evolutionary experts, the primitive grandmother of all birds "ran along the ground chasing flying insects which they nabbed with its teeth or front legs." In time, longer feathers on the front legs evolved to act as an insect net, and so

Figure #190. "LONG LIVE EVOLUTIONISM"

the legs simply became wings. Then the wings were used to make flapping leaps after insects. One wonders how and why educated men create such incredible fantasies. (The answer is found in Romans 1:18-23.)

Still more miracles are necessary. According to evolutionism, the lizards' forelimbs gradually changed into wings. Yet no one has ever found any fossils that show these in-between structures in any creature. Reptiles have always had four legs, scales and solid bones. Birds have always had two legs, two wings, beautiful feathers and hollow bones. To date no one has ever found a creature either alive or in the fossil record that is part reptile and part bird.

Recently, another bird was found. It is dated by evolutionists to be 75 million years older than Archaeopteryx. Therefore, Archaeopteryx could certainly not be the ancestor of the bird. Actually, evolutionists don't have any idea how the reptiles could have evolved into birds. They don't have any transitional forms to substantiate the theory they have concocted. But that doesn't stop them. You pick up any book on evolutionism, and Archaeopteryx is still presented as the best evidence.

Jumping Across a Gully.

At this point, one might ask what evolutionists plan to tell the generations of students who were duped into believing the transitional forms reported as fact in evolutionary textbooks but really never existed at all. I suppose nothing. No doubt it will be either ignored or forgotten as new mythological fantasies replace this one.

Would you believe there is now a bold new evolutionary idea too ridiculous to believe, yet it has already been around for some years? In spite of its unbelievable assumptions, it doesn't look like it will be leaving for some time.

The idea caught on because common sense dictates that it is wiser to make one long jump across a giant chasm than a series of small jumps. In other words, one can't jump across the Grand Canyon in small leaps — or even a giant leap for that matter. **(See fig. 191.)** Charles Darwin attempted to make the jump between one species to another in a series of gradual changes, and this is what most evolutionists have finally concluded to be incorrect because they can find no evidence. Therefore, the evolutionary community seems to have decided that it took only one long jump for one species to evolve into another. They admit that the infinite number of gaps in the fossil record simply do not allow for gradual changes. But their one-great leap theory of evolution is just as impossible as the idea that a

Figure #191. PUNCTUATED EQUILIBRIUM

Scene #3

person can get across the Grand Canyon in one giant leap. Keep in mind, it's not the leap that kills you, but the impact. The evolutionists can leap all they want, but their theory simply won't survive the impact of reality awaiting it.

Punctuated Equilibrium.

Many well-known evolutionists have risen to new realms of "reason" by attempting to jump across the chasm between species in one giant step. A scientist named Goldschmidt proposed this idea years ago. He claims that the reason there are no intermediate links found in the fossil record is because there are none to be found. (On this point, we fully agree with Mr. Goldschmidt.)

Yet Goldschmidt's solution is truly stranger than fiction. Supposedly two reptiles mated ... an egg was laid ... and when it hatched ... out popped Polly the parrot. **(See fig. #192.)** This happened with every type of creature in existence. This theory has been given the sophisticated name, "punctuated equilibrium." Now doesn't that sound a bit more "scientific"? I think its original name is more appropriate: "The Hopeful Monster Theory." Does this idea sound like a theory coming from brilliant educated men of science or a story from a pre-school children's reader?

Figure #192. POLLY, THE FREAK OF NATURE

Newsweek **Reports.**

> Though their existence provides the
> basis for paleontology, fossils have
> always been something of an embarrass-
> ment to evolutionists. The problem is
> one of "missing links": the fossil record
> is so littered with gaps that it takes a truly
> expert and imaginative eye to discern
> how one species could have evolved into
> another. Thus, the fossils lend credence
> to a new model of evolution called punc-
> tuated equilibrium.[38]

Thus the evolutionists admit that the fossil
record fails to document a single example of
evolutionism accomplishing a major transition
from one species to another, and hence offers no
evidence that the gradualistic model can be valid.

Monster Evolutionism.

The new theory is actually an old one that was
once totally scorned by the world's biologists.
Now it has been resurrected as credible because
there is no other direction in which evolutionists
can turn. Thus, we have now officially entered
the age of "monster evolutionism" or as it is more
respectfully labeled, "punctuated equilibrium."
It is as if evolutionism has suddenly developed a

case of the hiccups.

Consider what this theory is postulating. Suppose a dozen reptilian lizards were running around together. They have mutated massively, either as a result of some cosmic disturbance in the heavens or some other freak of nature. One day, one of them wakes up with green and purple feathers poking out and another having sprouted wings as if by magic. These two mate and, poof, you've got your first monster — or what has come to be called the bird. Now the offspring of these mutated lizards take to the air.

Not only is this ridiculous theory considered a possible explanation for the origin of birds — but every other species as well. This incredible theory speculates that every creature is just a deformed product of some cosmic mishap — monsters of one kind or another. Doesn't that give new purpose and meaning to your life? No wonder, with this kind of instruction in the public school system, there is such a rash of monster-like behavior. Students are only practicing what they are being taught to believe about themselves. They are descendants of the apes. Have you ever watched how apes get along with one another?

The Heart of Man is Deceptively Wicked.

How is it possible that educated men would

want to create such incredible fantasies?

> The wrath of God is being revealed from heaven against all the godlessness and wickedness of men who suppress the truth by their wickedness, since what may be known about God is plain to them, because God has made it plain to them. For since the creation of the world God's invisible qualities — his eternal power and divine nature — have been clearly seen, being understood from what has been made, so that men are without excuse. For although they knew God, they neither glorified him as God nor gave thanks to him, but their thinking became futile and their foolish hearts were darkened. Although they claimed to be wise, they became fools and exchanged the glory of the immortal God for images made to look like mortal man and birds and animals and reptiles (Rom. 1:18-23).

How is it possible for intelligent people to turn to such illogical fantasies for the origin of life? People are open to gross deception when they reject what they know about God. Instead of looking to Him as the Creator and Sustainer of life, they see themselves as the center of the universe. As a result, they begin to invent "gods" that are convenient projections of their self-centeredness. Thus, man substitutes the truth about God with a fantasy of his own imagination in order to support his own self-centered lifestyle. The evolutionary exchange of the glory of God for images of birds, animals and reptiles (dinosaurs), is fossil foolery.

Chapter Forty-Five

The Doom of the Dragon

The Spirit of Leviathan.

The creature the Bible refers to as leviathan is now extinct. **(See fig. #193.)** But the spirit of leviathan lives on: pride. It is this spirit of arrogance which causes men to imagine they are mighty and invincible. This deceptive force inflates man's ego to enormous proportions, and tempts him to live a self-sufficient life. It is this spirit that leads man to believe he has no need of God, leaving him prey to the seductions of Satan. Evolutionists are used by Satan as pawns to perpetuate and spread delusion — any notion that leads away from God will do.

The spirit of pride rules much of the world. We have become a race of success addicts. Winning, at any cost — even at the expense of family and friends, has become the objective. Making it to the top of the honor roll, the corporate ladder, or the championship finals has become all-im-

Figure #193. LEVIATHAN OF THE SEA

portant for most today. This attitude has even infiltrated the Church. The deceptive spirit of leviathan, making us believe we are invincible, is prevalent everywhere.

The fall of man produced a drastic change in all of God's creation. And after the Noah's Flood, the animal kingdom was more aggressive as the creatures struggled to survive on a less hospitable Earth. By the time the book of Job was written, the creature leviathan was the largest, fiercest, and most dreaded animal known to man. He seemed invincible. He could neither be tamed nor captured. His reptilian armor was impenetrable.

The Last Leviathan: Satan.

The leviathan in Job was a real animal, presumably the largest and fiercest of all the dinosaurs. In his post-fall state, he symbolized the great power and pride of the wicked one, Satan. **(See fig. #194.)** Some of the scriptural references to leviathan could not literally apply to any animal. They apply ultimately to Satan alone.

In reading Job 41, it seems we alternately read about a powerful animal and a more powerful sinister spirit, as though God were describing both leviathan and Satan at the same time. The following statements and phrases, for example, though referring directly to the great animal,

Figure #194. SEVEN-HEADED LEVIATHAN

seem also to personify him as evil.

> Will he keep begging you for mercy?
> Will he speak to you with gentle
> words? Will he make an agreement
> with you for you to take him as your
> slave for life? Any hope of subduing
> him is false; the mere sight of him is
> overpowering. His chest is hard as
> rock, hard as a lower millstone. Noth-
> ing on earth is his equal — a creature
> without fear (Job 41:3,4,9,24,33).

Read the decisive conclusion in this last verse
of God's message to Job:

> He looks down on all that are haughty;

he is king over all that are proud (Job 41:34).

Such a statement could not be true of any animal, but it is true of Satan. That old serpent, the devil, can be called the king of all the proud, for he is the father of all pride. Only Satan has beheld all high things. He once was God's anointed cherub, the highest of all the angels, but he wanted to exalt his own throne above the throne of God, and God had to cast him out. The story is told more fully in Isaiah and Ezekiel.

> How you have fallen from heaven, O morning star, son of the dawn! You have been cast down to the earth, you who once laid low the nations! You said in your heart, 'I will ascend to heaven; I will raise my throne above the stars of God; I will sit enthroned on the mount of assembly, on the utmost heights of the sacred mountain. I will ascend above the tops of the clouds; I will make myself like the Most High.' But you are brought down to the grave, to the depths of the pit (Isa. 14:12-15).

The word of the LORD came to me:

"Son of man, take up a lament concerning the king of Tyre and say to him: 'This is what the Sovereign LORD says: 'You were the model of perfection, full of wisdom and perfect in beauty. You were in Eden, the garden of God; every precious stone adorned you: ruby, topaz and emerald, chrysolite, onyx and jasper, sapphire, turquoise and beryl. Your settings and mountings were made of gold; on the day you were created they were prepared. You were anointed as a guardian cherub, for so I ordained you. You were on the holy mount of God; you walked among the fiery stones. You were blameless in your ways from the day you were created till wickedness was found in you. Through your widespread trade you were filled with violence, and you sinned. So I drove you in disgrace from the mount of God, and I expelled you, O guardian cherub, from among the fiery stones. Your heart became proud on account of your beauty, and you corrupted your wisdom because of your splendor. So I threw you to the earth; I made a spectacle of you before kings. By your many sins and dishonest trade you have desecrated your sanctuaries. So I made a fire come out from you, and it consumed you, and I reduced you to ashes on the ground in the sight of all who were watching. All the nations who knew you are appalled at you; you have come to a horrible end and will be no more'" (Ezek. 28:11-19).

It is interesting to note the use of parallel meanings in these passages. The Isaiah passage is addressed both to the wicked king of Babylon and to the devilish one controlling him. The Ezekiel passage is addressed seemingly to the evil king of Tyre, but soon it becomes apparent the message goes beyond him to Satan. In Job, God's description of the fearful dragon, leviathan, applies more fully to Satan, who may have even been possessing its body, just as he had once used the serpent back in the Garden of Eden.

Reading Between the Lines.

By reviewing the book of Job and reading between the lines, we can quickly conclude that Satan was nearby, for it was he who caused Job's fiery trial. Satan's prideful and arrogant challenge of God in the heavenly gathering of the angelic creatures had initiated this entire spectacle. Thus, we can assume that at the end of the drama, Satan is still present somewhere, somehow, in some form. No doubt Job could sense the deadly presence of the evil one, who had been battling with God for his soul.

It is not certain how much Job knew regarding the demonic forces in the heavenlies, even after his battle when his testing was over. The Old Testament has little to offer to enlighten us on Satan's strategies. But we receive explicit knowledge in the New Testament from such passages as Ephesians 6.

Nevertheless, leviathan clearly symbolizes Satan. The Bible is explicit regarding Satan's future and end.

> In that day, the LORD will punish with his sword, his fierce, great and powerful sword, Leviathan the gliding serpent, Leviathan the coiling serpent; he will slay the monster of the sea (Isa. 27:1). **(See fig. #195.)**

Perhaps to foreshadow this end-time doom of Satan, God eliminated all real dragons from the earth. In effect, God was promising the extinction of Satan when He said His sword could reach behemoth, and again in Isaiah when he said

Figure #195. THE SLAYING OF THE LEVIATHAN

His "strong sword" would punish leviathan.

> It was you who split open the sea by your power; you broke the heads of the monster in the waters. It was you who crushed the heads of Leviathan and gave him as food to the creatures of the desert (Psa. 74:13,14).

Although God was speaking to Job, He was also announcing His victory over Satan, both concerning Job's suffering ordeal and in the age-long spiritual conflict that would continue for another several thousand years. Satan may doubt it, but his own doom is as certain as that of the dinosaurs.

Thus the extinction of the dinosaur — the dragons of the past — reveals the final destruction of Satan in the future.

> But you are brought down to the grave, to the depths of the pit (Isa. 14:15).

The dragon finally appears again in the last book of the Bible, not in his role as the "angel of light" (II Cor. 11:14), in which he has deceived multitudes, but in his real nature, as the ferocious dragon.

> And there was war in heaven. Michael and his angels fought against the dragon, and the dragon and his angels

> fought back. But he was not strong
> enough, and they lost their place in
> heaven (Rev. 12:7,8).

No longer will Satan nor any of his angels be
able to enter God's presence in heaven to accuse
the people of God, as he did against Job and as
he continues to do in our day.

> The great dragon was hurled down —
> that ancient serpent called the devil, or
> Satan, who leads the whole world
> astray. He was hurled to the Earth, and
> his angels with him. Then I heard a
> loud voice in heaven say: "Now have
> come the salvation and the power and
> the kingdom of our God, and the
> authority of his Christ. For the accuser
> of our brothers, who accuses them be-
> fore our God day and night, has been
> hurled down" (Rev. 12:9,10).

This verse tells us Satan accuses us just as he did
Job, and that God may allow him to test us, as He
did Job. Christ allowed Satan to test Peter, "Simon,
Simon, Satan has asked to sift you as wheat. But I
have prayed for you, Simon, that your faith may not
fail. And when you have turned back, strengthen
your brothers" (Lk. 22:31,32).

Satan may accuse us and try us, but the Lord Jesus Christ is our defender!

> My dear children, I write this to you so that you will not sin. But if anybody does sin, we have one who speaks to the Father in our defense — Jesus Christ, the Righteous One. He is the atoning sacrifice for our sins, and not only for ours but also for the sins of the whole world (I Jn. 2:1,2).

Finally, all the testing will be over, and the great dragon will be destroyed.

> And I saw an angel coming down out of heaven, having the key to the Abyss and holding in his hand a great chain. He seized the dragon, that ancient serpent, who is the devil, or Satan, and bound him for a thousand years. He threw him into the Abyss, and locked and sealed it over him, to keep him from deceiving the nations anymore (Rev. 20:1-3).

This is not quite his final end, however. After the thousand-year reign of Christ and His saints over the Earth,

> He must be set free for a short time (Rev. 20:3).

After one final rebellion of men and devils, this conflict of the ages between God and Satan will be ended.

> And the devil, who deceived them, was thrown into the lake of burning sulfur, where the beast and the false prophet had been thrown. They will be tormented day and night for ever and ever (Rev. 20:10). **(See fig. #196.)**

In that day, all the saints will learn, as Job did,

Figure #196. THE END OF LEVIATHAN

that "our present sufferings are not worth comparing with the glory that will be revealed in us" (Rom. 8:18). We will "have heard of Job's perseverance and have seen what the Lord finally brought about. The Lord is full of compassion and mercy" (Jas. 5:11).

Thus the doom of the dragon (Satan) leviathan is sealed and certain. For the **KING OF KINGS, CHRIST JESUS** has prophesied his end. Those who have not turned their lives over to Christ will, like the dragon, be cast into the eternal punishment, the penitentiary of the universe.

> If anyone's name was not found written in the book of life, he was thrown into the lake of fire (Rev. 20:15).

> The unbelieving ... their place will be in the fiery lake of burning sulfur. This is the second death (Rev. 21:8).

Only those who have humbled themselves, repented of sin, and made Christ the Lord and Savior of their lives will live with the King of the Universe forever.

> Blessed and holy are those who have part in the first resurrection. The second death has no power over them, but

they will be priests of God and of Christ and will reign with Him (Rev. 20:6).

The Spirit and the bride say, "Come!" And let him who hears say, "Come!" Whoever is thirsty, let him come; and whoever wishes, let him take the free gift of the water of life (Rev. 22:17).

For God so loved the world that He gave His one and only Son, that whoever believes in Him shall not perish but have eternal life (Jn. 3:16).

Endnotes

1. For a look at the Pre-Flood world, see Volume IV of the Creation Science Series titled *The Canopy Theory — World That Was*.

2. *The Dallas Morning News*, Saturday, April 26, 1997.

3. *Modern Maturity*, "Dinosaur Dynasty," October/November 1986.

4. *The Dallas Morning News*, Saturday, August 9, 1986.

5. For additional understanding of giantism, refer to Volume IV of the Creation Science Series titled *The Canopy Theory — World That Was*. See ad at end of book.

6. Charles Darwin, "On the Imperfection of the Geological Record," Chapter X, *On the Origin of Species*, J.M. Dent and Sons Ltd., London, 1971, pp. 292-293.

7. Personal letter (written April 10, 1979) from Dr. Colin Patterson, senior paleontologist at the British Museum of Natural History in London, to Luther D. Sunderland; as quoted in *Darwin's Enigma* by Luther D. Sunderland, Master Books, San Diego, 1984, p. 89.

8. A complete explanation of the gap theory and its underlying problems will be covered in a future volume of the Creation Science Series.

9. Volume VI of the Creation Science Series titled *The Genesis Flood — Continents in Collision* covers the entire subject of the biblical Flood, and its massive worldwide destructive nature.

10. Again, it must be mentioned that the ancient dates ascribed by evolutionists to the geological layers are based on a hypothetical theory full of assumptions never shown to be fact. The complete exposure of the fallacies of evolutionary rock and fossil dating are covered in Volume VIII and IX of the Creation Science Series titled *The Birth of Planet Earth and the Age of the Universe* and The *Dismantling of Evolutionism's Sacred Cow: Radiometric Dating*.

11. The books titled *Tracing Those Incredible Dinosaurs* by John Morris and *Dinosaur: Scientific Evidences That Dinosaurs and Men Walked Together* by Carl Baugh, Ph.D. with Clifford A. Wilson, Ph.D. give a thorough presentation and documentation of the prints. The dinosaur prints were authenticated years ago; however, evolutionists have been reluctant to authenticate the human prints since the two life forms are supposed to be separated by 65 million years of geologic time —

according to theory of evolutionism.

12. *Moscow News*, 1983, No. 24, p.10.

13. *Sydney Morning Herald*, Australia, November 21, 1983, p. 1, late edition. Fuller details are given in the *Moscow News*, 1983, No. 24, p. 10, Cr. V. Rubtsov.

14. For a complete account of these hoaxes, see Volume X of the Creation Science Series titled *The ABCs of Evolutionism — Ape-Man, Batman, Catwoman and Other Evolutionary Fantasies (The Rest of the Story)*.

15. For an in-depth study of the size and storage capacity of the Ark, see Volume VI of the Creation Science Series titled *The Genesis Flood — Continents in Collision*.

16. Paul S. Taylor, *The Great Dinosaur Mystery and the Bible*, Denver: Accent, 1987, 1989, p, 36. Paul S. Taylor and Films for Christ.

17. "The Great Dinosaur Mystery" motion picture, 1979, Paul S. Taylor and Eden Films (Films for Christ).

18. Henry M. Morris, *The Defender's Study Bible* note on Genesis 10:8, p. 29.

19. *Encyclopedia Britannica*, 1962, Vol. 10, p. 359.

20. Bill Cooper, "Anglo-Saxon Dinosaurs as Described in Early Historical Records," Pamphlet No. 280, Creation Science Movement, Portsmouth, UK, 1992.

21. *Encyclopedia Britannica*, 1962, Vol. 10, p. 359.

22. *Encyclopedia Britannica*, 1962, Vol. 10, p. 359.

23. Paul S. Taylor, *The Great Dinosaur Mystery and the Bible,* Denver, Accent, 1987, 1989, p. 43.

24. *National Geographic*, October 1967.

25. Paul S. Taylor, *The Great Dinosaur Mystery and the Bible,* Denver: Accent, 1987, 1989, p. 41.

26. W. Bölsche, *Drachen. Sage und Naturwissenschaft,* Stuttgart, Kosmos, 1929.

27. Paul S. Taylor, *The Great Dinosaur Mystery and the Bible,* Denver, Accent, 1987, 1989, p. 40.

28. Dr. Peter Wellnhofer, *The Illustrated Encyclopedia of Pterosaurs,* Salamander Books Ltd., 1991, p. 8.

29. Duane T. Gish, Ph.D., *Dinosaurs by Design*, Creation-Life Publishing Inc., p. 16.

30. Paul S. Taylor, *The Great Dinosaur Mystery and the Bible*, Denver, Accent, 1987, 1989, p. 46.

31. Duane T. Gish, Ph.D., *Dinosaurs by Design,* Creation-Life Publishing Inc., p. 86.

32. Ian Taylor, *In the Minds of Men*, Toronto, TFE Publishing, 1984, p. 210.

33. *Edmonton Journal*, October 26, 1987, and *Saturday Night*, August 1989, Vol. 104, No. 8,

pp. 16-19.

34. *Time*, September 22, 1986, p. 84 and J.F. Basinger, "Our 'Tropical' Arctic," *Canadian Geographic*, 1986-7, Vol. 106, No. 6, pp. 28-37.

35. Alan Charig, *A New Look at the Dinosaurs*, p. 150.

36. For a complete study of the Ice Age see Volume VI of the Creation Science Series titled *The Original Star Wars and the Age of Ice*.

37. The canopy theory is covered in Volume IV of the Creation Series titled *The Canopy Theory — World That Was*.

38. *Newsweek*, December 7, 1981, p. 114.

Bibliography

An Educational Coloring Book of Prehistoric Birds. Medinah, IL: Spizzirri Publishing Co. Inc., 1981.

Baker, Mace. *Dinosaurs*. Redding, CA: New Century Books, 1991.

Baugh, Carl E. *Dinosaur*. Orange, CA: Promise Publishing Co., 1987.

Beierle, Fredrick P. *Man, Dinosaurs and History*. Prosser, WA: Perfect Printing, 1977.

Bird, Roland T. *Bones for Barnum Brown*. Fort Worth, TX: Texas Christian University Press, 1985.

Bristow, Pamela. *All Color World of Prehistoric Animals*. Hong Kong: Octopus Books Limited, 1980.

Carr, Archie. *The Reptiles*. New York: Time Incorporated, 1963.

Czerkas, Sylvia J. and Stephan A. Czerkas. *Dinosaurs, A Global View*. New York: Mallard Press, 1991.

Czerkas, Sylvia J. and Everett C. Olson. *Dinosaurs Past and Present*. Los Angeles,

CA: The Natural History Museum Foundation, 1987.

Dixon, Dougal. *The Illustrated Dinosaur Encyclopedia*. New York: Gallery Books, 1988.

_____. *Time Exposure*. New: Beaufort Books Inc., 1984.

Dixon, Dougal and Barry Cox, R.J.G. Savage, Brian Gardiner. *The Macmillan Illustrated Encyclopedia of Dinosaurs and Prehistoric Animals, A Visual Who's Who of Prehistoric Life*. New York: Macmillan Publishing Company, 1988.

Dougherty D.C., Dr. C.N. *Valley of the Giants*. Cleburne, TX: Bennett Printing Company, 1977.

Fields, Wilbur. *Paluxy River Exploration*. Published 1980. Not copyrighted.

Fricke, Hans. *Coelacanths: The Fish That Time Forgot*. National Geographic, June 1988, pp. 824-838

Ganeri, Anita. *Amazing Prehistoric Facts*. New York: Mallard Press, 1991.

Gardom, Tim with Angela Milner. *The Book of Dinosaurs, The Natural History Museum Guide*. Rocklin, CA: Prima Publishing, 1993.

Gillette, David D. *Seismosaurus, The Earth Shaker*. New York: Columbia University Press, 1994.

Gish, Ph.D., Duane T. *Dinosaurs by Design*. Colorado Springs, CO: Creation-Life Publishers Inc., 1992.

_____. *Dinosaurs: Those Terrible Lizards*. San Diego, CA: Creation-Life Publishers Inc., 1977.

Halstead, L.B. and Jenny Halstead. *Dinosaurs*. Dorset, U.K.: Blandford Books Ltd., 1981.

Ham, Ken. *Dinosaurs and the Bible*. Florence, KY: Answers in Genesis, 1993.

Heritage, John. *The Mysterious World of Dinosaurs*. London, WI: Octopus Books Limited, 1980.

Lambert, David. *The Dinosaur Data Book*. New York: Avon Books, 1990.

_____. *The Ultimate Dinosaur Book*. New York: Dorling Kindersley Inc., 1993.

Lindsay, William. *American Museum of Natural History, Barosaurus*. New York: Dorling Kindersley Inc., 1992.

_____. *The Great Dinosaur Atlas*. London, WC2E 8PS: Dorling Kindersley Limited, 1992.

Lockley, Martin and Adrian P. Hunt. *Dinosaur Tracks, and Other Fossil Footprints of the Western United States*. New York: Columbia University Press, 1995.

Moore, Ruth. *Evolution*. New York: Time

Incorporated, 1962.

Morris, Henry M. *The Remarkable Record of Job.* Grand Rapids, MI: Baker Book House, 1988.

Morris, John. *Tracking Those Incredible Dinosaurs and the People Who Knew Them.* San Diego, CA: CLP Publishers, 1980.

Norman Ph.D., David and Angela Milner Ph.D. *Dinosaur.* New York: Alfred A. Knopf Inc., 1989.

Norman, Dr. David. *The Prehistoric World of the Dinosaur.* New York: Gallery Books, 1988.

Parker, Steve. *Dinosaurs and How They Lived.* New York: Dorling Kindersley, 1991.

_____. *Prehistoric Life.* New York: Dorling Kindersley, 1991.

Petersen, Dennis R. *Unlocking the Mysteries of Creation.* South Lake Tahoe, CA: Christian Equippers Int'l., 1986.

Philips, Phil. *Dinosaurs, the Bible, Barney and Beyond.* Lancaster, PA: Starburst Inc., 1994.

Psihoyos, Louie with John Knoebber. *Hunting Dinosaurs.* New York: Random House Inc., 1994.

Segraves, Kelly L. *Dinosaur Dilemma.* San Diego, CA: Beta Books, 1977.

_____. *The Great Dinosaur Mistake.* San Diego, CA: Beta Books, 1975.

Spinar, Prof. Zdenek V. and Dr. Philip J. Currie.

The Great Dinosaurs. Stamford, CT: Longmeadow Press, 1994.

Stout, William. *The Dinosaurs*. New York: Bantam Books, 1981.

Taylor, Paul S. and Films For Christ Association. *The Great Dinosaur Mystery and the Bible*. El Cajon, CA: Master Books, 1987.

Time-Life Books. *Mysterious Creatures*. Alexandria, VA, 1988.

Wellnhofer, Dr. Peter. *The Illustrated Encyclopedia of Pterosaurs*. London: Salamander Book Limited, 1991.

Wilford, John Noble. *The Riddle of the Dinosaur*. New York: Alfred A. Knopf Inc., 1985.

Wilkes, Angela. *The Big Book of Dinosaurs*. New York: Dorling Kindersley, 1994.

Whitecomb, John C. and Henry M. Morris. *The Genesis Flood*. Grand Rapids, MI, 1961.

_____ . *The World That Perished*. Grand Rapids, MI: Baker Book House, 1988.

Video: *The Great Dinosaur Mystery*. Films For Christ Association, Mesa, AZ, 1987.

Illustrations